Travel

S0-BFA-480

JORDAN

MOIRA McCROSSAN & HUGH TAYLOR

NEW
HOLLAND

NEW
HOLLAND

★★★ Highly recommended
★★ Recommended
★ See if you can

Third edition published in 2011
by New Holland Publishers (UK) Ltd
London • Cape Town • Sydney • Auckland
10 9 8 7 6 5 4 3 2 1
website: www.newhollandpublishers.com

Garfield House, 86 Edgware Road
London W2 2EA, United Kingdom

80 McKenzie Street
Cape Town 8001, South Africa

Unit 1, 66 Gibbes Street
Chatswood NSW 2067, Australia

218 Lake Road, Northcote
Auckland, New Zealand

Distributed in the USA by
The Globe Pequot Press, Connecticut

ISBN 978 1 78009 027 6

This guidebook has been written by independent authors and
updaters. The information therein represents their impartial
opinion, and neither they nor the publishers accept payment
in return for including in the book or writing more favourable
reviews of any of the establishments. Whilst every effort has
been made to ensure that this guidebook is as accurate and
up to date as possible, please be aware that the facts quoted
are subject to change, particularly the price of food, transport
and accommodation. The Publisher accepts no responsibility
or liability for any loss, injury or inconvenience incurred by
readers or travellers using this guide.

Publishing Manager: Thea Grobbelaar
DTP Cartographic Manager: Genené Hart
Editors: Thea Grobbelaar, Lorissa Bouwer
Design and DTP: Nicole Bannister
Cartographers: Reneé Spocter, Luyolo Ndlotyeni,
Nicole Bannister
Picture Researchers: Felicia Apollis, Shavonne Govender
Consultant: Dave Saunders

Reproduction by Resolution, Cape Town
Printed and bound by Times Offset (M) Sdn. Bhd., Malaysia

Acknowledgements:
Hugh Taylor and Moira McCrossan would like to thank the
following for their assistance: David Symes, Jordan Tourist
Board; Chris Johnson, RSCN; Mohammed Hallak, Rent a
Reliable Car; Charl al-Twal, Mariam Hotel Madaba;
Saleem Ali, Jordan Tracks, Wadi Rum; Sameer Al-Momani,
Stationmaster, Hejaz Railway, Amman; Emma Hill and
Tiggy Dean, Hill and Dean PR; Marissa Garcia Olm,
Kempinski Ishatar; Ursula Necknig, Mövenpick Hotels

Keep us Current
Information in travel guides is apt to change, which is why
we regularly update our guides. We'd be grateful to receive
feedback if you've noted something we should include in
our updates. If you have new information, please share it
with us by writing to the Publishing Manager, Globetrotter,
at the office nearest to you (addresses on this page). The
most significant contribution to each new edition will
receive a free copy of the updated guide.

Cover: *Hiking across the desert.*
Title page: *Desert sunset, Wadi Rum.*

CONTENTS

1
Introducing
Jordan

For a country that is 90% desert Jordan has more to offer than most other destinations. Since the dawn of time it has been an international crossroads on major trade routes from Africa to the Far East. The nomadic ancestors of the Arab and Jewish people settled here. Jordan was the main stage for many major historical events. The **Patriarch Abraham** settled here and **Lot**, his nephew, fled the destruction of **Sodom** and **Gomorrah**. **Moses** led the **Children of Israel** through Jordan on their journey to the **Promised Land**.

In the eastern and southern deserts are the fascinating remnants of the ancient **Islamic Umayyad Dynasty**. **Qasr Amra**, a bath house with important wall paintings, is a **World Heritage site**. Another World Heritage site, **Petra**, featured in *Indiana Jones and the Last Crusade*. David Lean's award-winning film *Lawrence of Arabia* was also shot in Jordan. This account of the **Great Arab Revolt** accurately portrayed the landscape of **Wadi Rum**, if not the actual events.

THE LAND

Jordan is a relatively small country, similar in size to Austria, Iceland or Portugal. However, despite its small size, it contains an incredible diversity of climate, terrain and landscape. Western Jordan enjoys a Mediterranean climate with hot, dry summers and cool, wet winters, while about 75% of the country has a desert climate. Jordan divides into three clear geographic areas: the **Jordan Valley**, the **Mountain Heights Plateau**, and the **eastern desert region**. Jordan's only outlet to

TOP ATTRACTIONS

*** Petra: ancient city and World Heritage site.
*** Jerash: finest Roman city in the Middle East.
*** Baptism Site: where John baptized Jesus.
*** Qasr Amra: Umayyad bath house and World Heritage site.
*** Umm ar-Rasas: Jordan's third World Heritage site famed for its mosaics.
*** Madaba Map: the oldest known map of the Holy Land.
*** Wadi Rum: outstanding natural landscape.
*** The Dead Sea: lowest point on Earth.

Opposite: *The Treasury, Petra's most beautiful monument.*

the sea is the **Gulf of Aqaba**. Landward, it is surrounded by Syria to the north, Iraq to the east, and by Saudi Arabia to the east and south. To the west is Israel and the occupied West Bank.

The Jordan Valley

The Jordan Valley, along the western border, is the country's most impressive natural feature. It is part of a vast geographical and geological fissure that runs north to south for around 6000km (3725 miles), from Lebanon and Syria through the Dead Sea, by Aqaba and the Red Sea to Mozambique. This fissure, named the **Great Rift Valley of Africa** by the Scottish explorer John Walter Gregory, was created 20 million years ago by shifting tectonic plates, which created a jagged rift with great mountains on either side of a low flat plain.

The Jordan River runs down from sources in the mountains in Syria into **Lake Tiberias**, 209m (686ft) below sea level. It ends at the **Dead Sea** which, at 418m (1371ft) below sea level, is the lowest point on the earth's surface. The river is now only 20–30m (66–98ft) wide here because large quantities of water have been diverted for irrigation. With no outlet to the ocean and intense evaporation, the Dead Sea is

the saltiest body of water on earth, with salinity of about 30%, or about eight times greater than the ocean. It is indeed dead since it sustains no plant or animal life apart from tiny quantities of bacteria and microbial fungi. Saturated with salt and minerals, the Dead Sea and the neighbouring **Zarqa Ma'in** hot springs are famous for their therapeutic mineral waters, drawing visitors from all over the world.

The northern part of the Jordan Valley, known as **the Ghor**, runs from the northern border down to the Dead Sea. Low lying and several degrees warmer than the rest of the country, the Ghor is Jordan's most fertile region with a year-round agricultural climate, making it the food bowl of Jordan.

South of the Dead Sea, the Jordan Valley runs on through **Wadi 'Araba**. This spectacular valley, 166km

(103 miles) long, is very hot, dry and sparsely populated. The Araba is arrestingly beautiful, with colourful cliffs and sharp mountain tops. Wadi 'Araba rises from 300m (984ft) below sea level at its northern end to 355m (1165ft) above sea level at **Jebel Risha**, and then drops down again to sea level at Aqaba.

The seaside city of Aqaba is Jordan's only access to the sea. It has some of the finest coral reefs in the world and a number of underwater wrecks, providing habitats for marine organisms. The rich marine life provides excellent snorkelling and diving opportunities.

Above: *Walk along the promenade at Aqaba and haggle with the skippers of glass-bottomed boats to get a good price.*
Opposite: *The intense heat of the sun causes evaporation which leaves salt deposits by the shores of the Dead Sea.*

The Mountain Heights Plateau

The highlands of Jordan, between the Jordan Valley and the plains of the eastern desert, stretch the length of the western part of the country. These areas receive the highest rainfall, and are the most richly vegetated in the country. Most of the main population centres are

COMPARATIVE CLIMATE CHART	AMMAN				PETRA				AQABA			
	WIN	SPR	SUM	AUT	WIN	SPR	SUM	AUT	WIN	SPR	SUM	AUT
	JAN	APR	JULY	OCT	JAN	APR	JULY	OCT	JAN	APR	JULY	OCT
MAX TEMP. °C	12	23	32	27	12	22	36	24	21	31	39	33
MIN TEMP. °C	3	9	18	14	4	11	18	14	9	17	25	20
MAX TEMP. °F	54	73	89	80	53	71	96	75	69	87	102	91
MIN TEMP. °F	27	48	64	57	39	51	64	57	48	62	77	68
RAINFALL mm	64	15	0	7	43	14	0	2	5	4	0	1
RAINFALL in	2.5	0.5	0	0.2	1.6	0.5	0	0	0.1	0.1	0	0

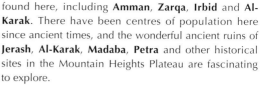

Below: *Although Petra is
commonly called the
Rose Red City, the sand-
stone is in fact a variety
of colours. Erosion of this
rock has exposed the
many varieties.*

found here, including **Amman**, **Zarqa**, **Irbid** and **Al-
Karak**. There have been centres of population here
since ancient times, and the wonderful ancient ruins of
Jerash, **Al-Karak**, **Madaba**, **Petra** and other historical
sites in the Mountain Heights Plateau are fascinating
to explore.

The region from **Umm Qais** in the north to **Ras
an-Naqab** in the south is intersected by a number of
valleys and river beds known as wadis. The height
above sea level in this area varies considerably, from
600m (1969ft) to about 1500m (4922ft), with temperature and rainfall patterns varying accordingly.

The part of the Mountain Heights Plateau known as
the northern highlands extends southwards from Umm
Qais to just north of Amman and has a typically Mediterranean climate and vegetation. Known historically
as the **Land of Gilead**, it is higher and cooler than the
southern part.

South and east of the northern highlands, between
the highlands and the eastern desert, are the **northern
steppes**. This area, from Irbid through **Mafraq** and
Madaba all the way south to Al-Karak, was formerly
covered in steppe vegetation; however, much of it is
now desert. In the south, the **Sharra highlands**, from
Ash Shawbak south to Ras
an-Naqab, is a high-altitude
plain with little annual rainfall and little vegetation.

The Eastern Desert or
Badia Region

This area makes up around
75% of Jordan. It stretches
into Syria, Iraq and Saudi
Arabia, with heights varying
between 600m (1969ft) and
900m (2953ft) above sea
level. It is mainly desert and
desert steppe, with a climate
which varies widely between

day and night, and between summer and winter. Daytime summer temperatures can be over 40°C (104°F), while winter nights are very cold and windy. Rainfall is minimal throughout the year, averaging less than 50mm (1.97in) annually. The regions of the **Badia** (or desert) vary considerably in geological formation.

The **northern Basalt Desert**, which extends into Syria and Saudi Arabia, has volcanic formations, characterized by the black basalt boulders which cover the landscape. East of the Basalt Desert, the **Rweishid Desert** is an undulating limestone plateau stretching to the border with Iraq. This supports some grassland and agriculture. Northeast of Amman, the **Eastern Desert** is crossed by a multitude of vegetated wadis, and includes the **Azraq Oasis** and the **Shaumari Wildlife Reserve**.

To the south of Amman is the **Central Desert**. **Al-Jafr Basin**, south of the Central Desert, is crossed by a number of broad, sparsely vegetated wadis. South of al-Jafr and east of the **Rum Desert**, **al-Mudawwara Desert** has lone hills and low, rocky mountains with broad, sandy wadis in between.

The most famous desert in Jordan is the Rum Desert, home of the wondrous **Wadi Rum** landscape. Towering mesas and sand dunes produce one of the most fantastic desert locations in the world, qualifying it to feature in the film **The Red Planet** as the surface of Mars.

Plant Life

Known in the Bible as the '**land of milk and honey**', Jordan has been renowned historically for its luxurious vegetation. During the 20th century, however, problems such as desertification and drought have damaged Jordan's natural habitat. Fortunately, Jordanians are now working to reverse the decline of their beautiful natural heritage. Nevertheless, the Kingdom retains a rich diversity of plant life.

Above: The famous red sand dunes make Wadi Rum one of the most fantastic desert locations in the world.

THE WHITE ORYX

This majestic beast may have been the origin of the **unicorn legends**. In Hebrew it is called re'em, which is translated to 'unicorn' in the King James Bible. In addition, when viewed in profile the oryx appears to have just one horn. It was hunted to extinction by 1972 but an extensive breeding program with animals held in zoos has saved the species, which has now been reintroduced to the wild.

Above: *The ibex is a wild mountain goat with two large horns that curve over its back.*

Spring is the best time to see flowers in Jordan, and from February to May the display of flowering plants in many regions is dazzling. More than 2000 species of plants grow in Jordan, and the variety of the country's geography and climate is reflected in its flora. Most species, however, depend heavily on the winter rains, without which Jordan's display of flowers can be much depleted. The most famous of Jordan's wild flowers is the **national flower**, the **black iris**.

The highlands of Jordan host forests of **oak** and **pine**, as well as **pistachio** and **cinnabar trees**. **Olive**, **eucalyptus** and **cedar** trees thrive throughout the highlands and in the Jordan Valley. Species of shrubs can be found throughout Jordan, since the dry climate is well suited to shrub trees, which require less water. Many small shrubs thrive in the Badia, providing grazing for the goats of local Bedouin tribes.

Wildlife

Jordan has about 70 species and subspecies of mammals, along with 73 reptile species. In the harsh conditions of the desert only the hardiest and most adaptable creatures survive. These are mainly **insects**, **lizards**, and **small mammals**. However, a number of larger mammals, including the **Asiatic jackal**, **desert fox**, **striped hyena**, **wolf**, **camel**, **rabbit** and **sand rat** roam the desert. The **white oryx**, which was hunted almost to extinction, lives on the open plains, while the **mountain ibex** is found among rocky, mountainous crags.

Jordan's varied habitats encourage a wide variety of bird species – both year-round residents and migratory visitors. About 150 species are indigenous to Jordan but many more pass through. Jordan lies on one of the world's major bird migration routes between Africa and Eurasia. Before the waters of Azraq Reserve diminished, as many as 200,000 birds, including **spoonbills**, **white pelicans**, **egrets**, **terns** and **gulls**, would congregate there during the migratory season. The numbers of migrants have decreased, yet even today up to 220 migratory species pass through Jordan on their journey north or south.

There are about 20 species of freshwater fish in Jordan's rivers and streams, while around 1000 species of fish swim in the rich waters of the Gulf of Aqaba. On the sandy shores, creatures such as the **ghost crab**, **sand-hoppers** and **mole crab** scuttle about, while the plethora of marine life includes starfish, sea cucumbers, crabs, shrimps, sea urchins, many species of fish and several worms that burrow into the sandy sea bottom. Several species of eel make their home in the gulf's grass beds, where one can also find **sea horses** and **pipefishes**.

The coral reefs of the Gulf of Aqaba are unmatched in the world for diving. Around 100 varieties of **stony coral** are found, mainly in shallow waters, as the **algae** that live within them require light for photosynthesis. Many hundreds of fish species dart among the reefs, eating the algae that grow on the coral.

HISTORY IN BRIEF

At the crossroads of the **Middle East**, where trade routes and armies have converged from **Asia**, **Africa** and **Europe** over the centuries, Jordan has been home to some of the earliest human settlements and many of the world's great civilizations.

Neolithic Period

In the Neolithic period (c. 8500–4500BCE), agriculture, pottery making and goat herding in settled communities replaced the hunter-gatherers of earlier times. At **Ein Ghazal** in Amman, archaeologists have found one of the world's oldest statues. Just over one metre high, it is of a woman with huge eyes, skinny arms, knobbly knees and carefully depicted toes.

THE SIX DAY WAR

This was also known as the 1967 Arab-Israeli war. It was precipitated by Israel because of their territorial ambitions regarding Jerusalem and the West Bank. They launched a pre-emptive attack on Egypt, and Jordan in turn attacked Israel. It ended with Israel controlling the West Bank, Gaza, the Sinai Peninsula and the Golan Heights. Despite UN Security Council Resolution 242, which called for Israel to withdraw from territories captured during the war, they are still in occupation of most of the land.

Below: *An effigy of T E Lawrence (Lawrence of Arabia), the British Army officer who fought with the Arabs during the Great Revolt.*

HISTORICAL CALENDAR

200,000–8000BCE First signs of human habitation date from the Palaeolithic Era (Stone Age).
1200–550BCE The Iron Age, when most of the events in the Old Testament took place.
311–63BCE Hellenistic Period.
312BCE to 112CE Nabatean Period.
63BCE–330CE Roman Period.
324–640CE Byzantine Period.
640–1099 Islamic Conquest.
1100–1260 The Crusades.
1174–1263 Ayyubid Period.
1263–1516 Mameluke Period.
1516–1918 Ottoman Period. Four hundred years of Turkish rule.
1916–1918 The Arab Revolt.
1916 The Sykes-Picot Agreement.
1917 The Balfour Declaration.
1920 Britain gains control of Palestine but recognizes Transjordan as an independent state under its protection.

1946 The British mandate over Palestine ends and Transjordan gains independence.
1947 The Dead Sea Scrolls are discovered in Qumran, Jordan.
1948 Arab-Israeli War.
1949 Transjordan is renamed the Hashemite Kingdom of Jordan.
1950 Jordan annexes the West Bank area of Arab Palestine, including East Jerusalem.
1951 King Abdullah is assassinated at the Al-Aqsa Mosque in Jerusalem on 20 July and is succeeded by his son, Prince Talal.
1952 King Hussein succeeds to the throne on the abdication of his father, King Talal.
1967 The Six Day War and the loss of East Jerusalem and the West Bank to Israel.
1970 Black September War against the PLO resulting in

their expulsion from Jordan and relocation in Lebanon.
1973 The fourth Arab-Israeli or 'Yom Kippur' War.
1988 King Hussein backs the Palestinian Intefada against Israel and renounces Jordan's claim to sovereignty over the West Bank in favour of the PLO.
1994 Jordan and Israel sign a peace treaty.
1996 Signing of a Trade Treaty by Jordan and Israel.
1998 King Hussein travels to the USA to receive cancer treatment.
1999 King Abdullah II succeeds his father, King Hussein, who died on 7 February.
2003 Faisal al-Fayez is appointed prime minister after the resignation of his predecessor.
2005 The government resigns and Adnan Badran is appointed prime minister of Jordan.

Chalcolithic Period

During the Chalcolithic period (c. 4500–3200BCE), copper was smelted for the first time and used for axes, arrowheads and hooks.

Early Bronze Age (c. 3200–1200BCE)

In 1482BCE, the **Egyptian Pharaoh** took over **Canaan** (**Palestine**, **Jordan** and **Syria**). Around 1200BCE, the main cities of Palestine and Jordan were destroyed, possibly by the mysterious 'Sea Peoples' from the **Aegean** and **Anatolia**. The **Israelites** may have been another cause of the devastation in Palestine. They are believed to have destroyed many Canaanite towns including **Ariha** (**Jericho**), **Ai** and **Hazor**.

WADIS

'Wadi' is an Arabic word for a dry river bed. They tend to be deep with steep walls rather like canyons and can be difficult to cross. During times of heavy rain they can fill up with water and at certain times can be dangerous to cross because of the risk of flash floods.

Left: Archaeologists continue to excavate the ruins in Jordan.

The Iron Age (c. 1200–332BCE)

This period saw the development of three new kingdoms in Jordan: **Edom** in the south, **Moab** in central Jordan, and **Ammon** in the northern mountain areas. The Edomites were skilled in copper mining and smelting. The Kingdom of Moab covered the centre of Jordan, and its capital cities were at **Al-Karak** and **Dhiban**. The Kingdom of Ammon developed agriculture and trade, as well as an organized defence policy with a series of fortresses. The wealth of these kingdoms made them targets for raids or even conquest by the neighbouring Israelites and the **Assyrians**.

The Assyrian Empire was followed by the **Babylonian Empire**, which gave way in 539BCE to the more organized life and prosperity of the **Persian Empire**. In 332BCE, **Alexander the Great** established Greek control over Jordan.

The Hellenistic Period

The Greeks founded new cities in Jordan and renamed others. Only fragments survive from the Hellenistic period, the most spectacular remains being **Iraq al-Amir**, just west of modern-day Amman. The **Qasr al-Abd** ('**Castle of the Slave**') there is constructed of very large stones, some of which have sculpted figures of lions and eagles.

THE MESHA STELE

King Mesha of Moab had this black basalt stele erected in 850BCE to record his victory over the Israelites. It was discovered by a German missionary in 1868 at Dhiban and arrangements were made for its purchase. Before this could be completed, locals broke it into several pieces. Fortunately a cast had been made and both it and the rebuilt stone are now in the Louvre in Paris.

ABRAHAM

The first Patriarch, Abraham, is the common ancestor of both the Jewish and Arab peoples. From his son, Isaac, and his grandson, Jacob, descended the Twelve Tribes of Israel. Another son, Ishmael, is regarded by both Islamic and Jewish traditions as the ancestor of the Prophet Mohammed. Originally from the City of Ur in Mesopotamia (Iraq), he moved with his followers to Canaan and settled near the Jordan River.

Before Alexander's conquest, a nomadic tribe known as the **Nabateans** had gradually begun migrating to Jordan from **Arabia**. Their capital city was the legendary **Petra**, which is today Jordan's most famous tourist attraction. Throughout much of the 3rd century BCE, the **Ptolemies** and the **Seleucids** warred over control of Jordan, with the Seleucids eventually emerging victorious in 198BCE.

The Age of Rome

Pompey's conquest of Jordan, Syria and Palestine in 63BCE inaugurated a period of Roman control, which would last four centuries.

In northern Jordan, the Greek cities of **Philadelphia** (Amman), **Gerasa** (Jerash) and **Gadara** (Umm Qais) joined with other cities in Palestine and southern Syria to form the **Decapolis League**, a confederation linked by bonds of economic and cultural interest. Of these, **Jerash** appears to have been the most splendid. It was one of the greatest provincial cities in Rome's empire.

Christendom and the Byzantines

The Byzantine period dates from 324CE, when the **Emperor Constantine I** founded **Constantinople** (present-day Istanbul) as the capital of the **Eastern Roman Empire**. **Christianity** gradually became the accepted religion of the area in the 4th century, and churches were built throughout Jordan.

The Islamic Periods and the Crusades

From 630CE the new faith of **Islam** spread rapidly throughout the Middle East and North Africa. For countless years marauding Bedouin tribesmen had raided the north. Now, however, united by a common faith, it took the Arabs only ten years to dismantle Byzantine control. In 636CE, the **Muslim** armies won a decisive battle against the Byzantines on the banks of the **Yarmuk River**. As Islam spread, the **Arabic** language gradually came to supplant Greek as the main language.

THE DECAPOLIS

This was a group of ten cities in Syria and Judea linked because of their Greek and Roman culture and language. They were located on the Roman Empire's eastern frontier in what is now the northwest of Jordan, the northeast of Israel and the southwest of Syria. This was not a formal political unit and each city had a large measure of autonomy.

Umayyad Empire

In 661CE the Muslims declared **Damascus** the capital of the Umayyad Empire. Jordan prospered during the Umayyad period (661–750CE) on account of its closeness to the capital and its strategic position on the pilgrim route to the holy Muslim sites.

When the Umayyads were defeated by the **Abbasids** three years later, they established their capital in faraway **Baghdad**. The Umayyads left an enduring legacy in the caravan stops (**caravanserais**) and palaces in the eastern Jordanian desert, collectively known as the '**Desert Castles**'.

Fatimids

In 969CE, the Fatimids of Egypt took control of Jordan and struggled over it with various Syrian factions for about two centuries. At the beginning of the 12th century, the **Crusades** began with a plea for help from the Emperor of Constantinople to his Christian European brothers. His city, the last bastion of Byzantine Christendom, was under threat of attack by the **Muslim Turks**. This resulted in the conquest of Jerusalem by Christian forces and the establishment of a series of fortresses in Jordan to protect the route to **Jerusalem**. However, Jerusalem was taken back in 1187 by the Muslim commander **Salah al-Din Yusuf Ibn Ayyub** (**Saladin**) at the **Battle of Hittin**.

SALADIN

Yusuf Ibn Ayyub was a Kurd from northern Iraq who became a Syrian warrior general and was known as Salah al-Din, which means 'The Righteousness of the Faith'. He was the founder of the Ayyubid dynasty that ruled Egypt and Syria, the Hejaz, Iraq, Mecca and Yemen, but is best remembered for finally defeating and expelling the Crusaders from the Middle East. His tomb is in a garden just outside the Umayyad Mosque in Damascus.

Below: *Qasr al-Azraq, the desert headquarters of Lawrence of Arabia during the Great Arab Revolt.*

Ayyubids and Mamelukes

Saladin founded the **Ayyubid dynasty**, which ruled much of Syria, Egypt and Jordan for the next 80 years. The **Mamelukes**, who were from Central Asia and the Caucasus, seized power in 1260 and ruled Egypt and later Jordan and Syria. The unification of Syria, Egypt and Jordan under the Ayyubids and Mamelukes led to another period of prosperity for Jordan. Castles were constructed or rebuilt, and caravanserais were built to host pilgrims and strengthen lines of communication and trade until, in 1516, the Mamelukes were defeated by the **Ottoman Turks** and Jordan became a part of the Ottoman Empire and remained so for the next 400 years.

Above: *This copy of the Mesha Stele is in the museum at Madaba. The inscription records a victory over the Israelites in 850BCE.*

The Ottoman Empire

The Ottomans were primarily interested in Jordan for the pilgrimage route to **Mecca**. They built a series of square fortresses for pilgrims. The **Bedouins**, however, remained masters of the desert, continuing to live much as they had for hundreds of years.

The Great Arab Revolt

Much of the suffering of the peoples of the Middle East during the 20th century can be traced to the events surrounding **World War I**. The Ottoman Empire sided with the **Central Powers** against the **Allies**, while Arab nationalist groups had begun to rally behind the **Hashemite** banner of **Abdullah** and **Faisal**, sons of **Sharif Hussein bin Ali**. In 1916 the Great Arab Revolt against Ottoman discrimination was launched, with the promised support of the **British** for a unified kingdom for the Arab lands. However, the victors reneged on their promises, patching together instead a system of mandates.

The Making of Transjordan

The **Sykes-Picot Agreement** established the framework for the mandate system in the years following the war. The newly founded **League of Nations** awarded Britain mandates over **Transjordan**, **Palestine** and **Iraq**. **France** was given the mandate over **Syria**, **Lebanon** and **Damascus**. The British proclaimed **Emir Abdullah** ruler of the three districts, known collectively as Transjordan. The emir established the first centralized governmental system in what is now modern Jordan in 1921.

In 1923, Britain formally recognized the **Emirate of Transjordan** as a state under the leadership of Emir Abdullah. In 1925, the Aqaba and **Ma'an** districts of the **Hejaz** became part of Transjordan. Abdullah set up the **Arab Legion** to ensure the defence of the state.

In 1928 he put forward a constitution, which provided for a parliament known as the **Legislative Council**. Elections were held in 1929, bringing to power the first Legislative Council of 21 members. Between 1928 and 1946, a series of Anglo-Transjordanian treaties finally led to full independence for Transjordan. In 1946, the Transjordanian parliament proclaimed Abdullah king, while officially changing the name of the country to the **Hashemite Kingdom of Jordan**.

The 1948 Arab-Israeli War

The **UN General Assembly** decided in 1947 to partition Palestine. Following the proclamation of the state of Israel in 1948, Lebanon, Syria, Egypt and Iraq sent

THE BALFOUR DECLARATION

In 1917 the British Foreign Secretary, Arthur James Balfour, wrote to Lord Lionel Rothschild committing the British Government to the support of Zionist aspirations to create a national home for the Jewish people in Palestine. The Declaration went on to state that 'nothing shall be done which may prejudice the civil and religious rights of existing non-Jewish communities in Palestine'.

THE SYKES-PICOT AGREEMENT

This secret agreement was negotiated between the French and British governments in 1916 and basically defined how the two countries intended to carve up the Middle East. Britain would have control of the area now known as Jordan, Iraq and an area around Haifa, while the French would take Lebanon, Syria, southeast Turkey and northern Iraq. The treaty takes its name from the two negotiators, Mark Sykes and François Georges-Picot.

THE ISLAMIC CALENDAR

This is used by Muslims to determine the dates of Islamic holy days. Based on the lunar cycle, each year has 12 lunar months and some 354 days. The Gregorian calendar, used by the rest of the world, is based on the solar cycle and has 11 more days. Islamic holy days are fixed and are 11 days earlier each year in relation to the Gregorian calendar.

troops to join with Jordanian forces in order to defend the indigenous inhabitants of Palestine. The **1948 Arab-Israeli War** ended in mid-1949, and a series of armistice agreements were signed between the Arab parties and Israel at **Rhodes**. Jordan did not participate, but made peace with Israel directly.

Unification of the Two Banks

In December 1948, Palestinian leaders from the West Bank called for King Abdullah to unite the two banks of the Jordan into a single state. In 1950, elections were held for a new Jordanian parliament in which the Palestinian Arabs of the West Bank were equally represented. The Hashemite Kingdom of Jordan now included half a million refugees from **Jewish-occupied Palestine**. All the refugees automatically became citizens of Jordan, a right offered to all Palestinians who wished to claim it.

Below: *King Abdullah II and his father, the late King Hussein, appear together in posters like this all over Jordan.*

The Assassination of King Abdullah

In 1951 King Abdullah was killed by a lone gunman at **al-Aqsa Mosque**. His grandson, the young **Prince Hussein**, escaped death because the bullet ricocheted

off a medal on his chest. The Jordanian throne passed briefly to **Crown Prince Talal**, the late king's eldest son, who soon abdicated for health reasons in favour of his eldest son Prince Hussein. Prince Hussein could not officially take over the throne until he reached the age of 18. Therefore, a Regency Council was put into place until 1953.

Jordan in the 1950s

The 1950s were a period of tumultuous political upheaval throughout the Arab world, mainly due to the creation of the state of Israel and the loss of Palestine. The **Ba'th Party** originated in Syria and a branch of this pan-Arabist party remain in power in Syria today.

One of the key players in Arab politics during the 1950s and 1960s was Egyptian **President Nasser**. Coming to power in 1954, Nasser had great charisma. His pan-Arabic message especially appealed to the displaced Palestinians. His popularity grew enormously after the **Suez Crisis** of 1956, when he appeared to be the new Saladin, who would unify the Arabs and take back Palestine. However, instead of fostering unity, the rivalry between Nasser and the Ba'thists led to deep divisions between Arab states.

In an important development, King Hussein dismissed the British commanders of the Arab Legion in 1956, and terminated the **Anglo-Jordanian Treaty** in March of 1957. In 1958, five months after the formation of the Arab Federation, a federal union between Jordan and Iraq, a coup in Iraq shattered the Arab Federation and left Jordan isolated. King Hussein was forced to accept British military help and an American oil airlift.

Jordan in the 1960s

The 1960s were promising, as the economy started to take off. Jordan's **potash**, **phosphate** and **cement** industries were developed and an **oil refinery** was constructed. The country was linked by a network of highways, and a new educational system was introduced. In 1962, the Kingdom constructed its first national university, **Jordan University**, at **Jubeiha**, on the outskirts of Amman. Prior to the **1967 War**, Jordan witnessed higher rates of economic growth than most other developing countries. A thriving construction industry provided job opportunities for Jordanians, while tourism from Jerusalem, **Bethlehem**, and the many East Bank attractions provided the Kingdom with foreign exchange income.

THE PROPHET MOHAMMED

Mohammed was born in Mecca in 570CE and started receiving his revelations from God when he was 40. Initially he tried to convert the people of Mecca but met strong opposition from the establishment and was obliged to flee to **Medina**. This event is called the *Hijra*, or flight, and marks the start of the Islamic calendar. Mohammed was eventually recognized as a prophet and returned to Mecca two years before his death in 632CE.

The 1967 War

The mid-1960s also saw the rise of independent Palestinian **guerrilla groups**, the most notable of which was **Yasser Arafat's Fatah** movement. The Ba'thist Syrian government encouraged guerrilla raids into Israel from Lebanon or Jordan, prompting reprisals from the Israelis. This led to recriminations from the Arab countries when Jordan blocked the guerrillas. In the midst of this tension Israel launched a surprise attack on 5 June 1967, virtually eliminating the Egyptian air force in a single blow. After destroying the Egyptian air force, Israel had complete control of the skies. When the final UN ceasefire was imposed on 11 June, Israel had taken Egyptian **Sinai**, Syria's **Golan Heights** and what remained of Arab Palestine, the West Bank. As a result of

Above: *A Jordanian soldier stands guard outside the tomb of King Hussein in the Royal Palace Garden.*

the war, more than 300,000 Palestinian Arabs became refugees and fled to Jordan. Jordan's economy was dealt a severe blow. About 70% of Jordan's agricultural land was located in the West Bank, which produced 60–65% of its fruits and vegetables. Half of the Kingdom's industrial establishments were located in the West Bank, while the loss of Jerusalem and other religious sites devastated the tourist industry.

Diplomatic and Military Initiatives

On 22 November 1967, the UN Security Council unanimously passed **Resolution 242**, calling on Israel to withdraw from the areas it had occupied in the recent war, and for all countries in the Middle East to respect the rights of others 'to live in peace within secure and recognized boundaries'. Jordan accepted the resolution as a basis for negotiation.

In 1970 the United States sponsored the **Rogers Plan**, a six-point Arab peace plan along the lines of Resolution 242. Although Jordan and Egypt publicly accepted the plan, its rejection by Israel, Syria and the PLO doomed it to failure.

The Conflict of 1970

By 1970 moderate Palestinian leaders were unable to control extremist elements, who ambushed the king's motorcade and engaged in a series of hijackings. King Hussein brought in the army. The conflict reached a crisis in September when some 200 Syrian tanks, camouflaged as Palestinian Liberation Army tanks, crossed into Jordan. The Syrians were forced to retreat within three days, and in a brief campaign the Jordanian army ended the operation of Palestinian guerrillas in Amman.

Jordan in the 1970s

As political stability gradually returned, Jordan enjoyed exponential social and economic growth owing much to the oil boom in the Middle East. The Lebanese civil war in 1975 led to much of Beirut city's banking and insurance infrastructure relocating to Amman, fueling a boom in service industries. By the early 1980s, Amman had been transformed into one of the most dynamic Arab capitals.

In 1978, King Hussein decreed that a **National Consultative Council** be created to replace parliament temporarily and martial law was imposed. Between 1978 and 1984 three councils were formed, consisting of

---

SUNNIS AND SHI'ITES

Mohammed did not appoint a successor so in the century following his death Islam split into two sects. Simply explained, the sects were divided as to who should have succeeded the prophet. Shi'ites recognize Ali, Mohammed's cousin and son-in-law, as his rightful successor and Caliph. Sunnis, on the other hand, accept Abu Bakr, his father-in-law, and the two Caliphs that followed him.

Below: *The national flag of Jordan evolved from the flag of the Great Arab Revolt. It is the same as the Palestinian flag but with the addition of a seven-pointed star.*

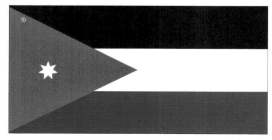

representatives appointed by King Hussein from various sectors of Jordanian society. These councils were a temporary measure while half of parliament's seats remained under Israeli occupation.

Palestinian nationalism continued to grow and in 1974 King Hussein, along with all the other Arab leaders, recognized the **Palestine Liberation Organization** as the 'sole, legitimate representative of the Palestinian people'.

Attention switched from the Arab-Israeli conflict to the **Arabian Gulf** in 1980 when war erupted between Iraq and **Iran**. Throughout the eight-year war, Jordan, along with the United States, France and Arabian Gulf countries, supported Iraq against the threat of Iranian expansionism.

Jordan's Democratic Renaissance

In recent years, Jordan has made remarkable progress toward establishing a pluralistic, organized political structure. In 1989, political reform began with free parliamentary elections with only East Bank constituencies. The new parliament emerged as a political force that exercised full legislative powers. In addition, the National Charter established the framework for organized political activity in the country, freedom of the press was enhanced and martial law was repealed.

The Gulf Crisis

In 1990, when Iraq invaded **Kuwait**, the conflict was extremely damaging to Jordan. With a population of only about three and a half million people at that time, it received over a

Below: *People in Jordan still use the donkey for everyday transport.*

million refugees. This influx led to an increased demand on **water supplies** and **infrastructure**, rising poverty and a sharp increase in **unemployment**. The international sanctions against Iraq, a major trading partner, created further economic difficulties for Jordan.

Above: *Amman has several bookshops selling the Qur'an and other Islamic texts.*

The Madrid Peace Process

At the Madrid Peace Conference in 1991, the Palestinian delegation negotiated with the Israelis directly for the first time. Two years later the PLO and Israel signed the **Declaration of Principles** (Oslo I), outlining a negotiating framework. In 1994, King Hussein and Israeli **Prime Minister Rabin** signed the **Washington Declaration** and soon after, at the southern border crossing of Wadi 'Araba, the **Jordan-Israel Peace Treaty** was signed. The treaty guaranteed Jordan the restoration of its occupied land and an equitable share of water from the Yarmouk and Jordan rivers. Following the treaty various agreements were reached establishing mutually beneficial arrangements for **trade**, **transportation**, **tourism**, **communications** and **energy** among other things.

THE TRAGEDY OF PALESTINE

After the war, in the wake of the Holocaust, thousands of displaced Jews emigrated to Palestine, while Jewish groups such as the **Irgun** waged a campaign of terror against the British. When the British mandate ended, the United Nations partitioned Palestine into an Arab state and a Jewish state allocating more than half the territory, including the valuable coastal strip, to the Jews, who owned about 6% of the land. Conflict was inevitable.

GOVERNMENT AND ECONOMY

Jordan is a **constitutional monarchy** with representative government. The reigning monarch, **King Abdullah II bin Al-Hussein**, exercises his executive authority through the prime minister and the cabinet which he appoints. They are responsible to the elected **House of Deputies** which, along with the **House of Notables** (Senate), constitutes the legislative branch of the government.

In February 2011, in the wake of the uprisings that toppled the regimes in Tunisia and Egypt, and following peaceful demonstrations in Jordan, King Abdulah dismissed his cabinet and appointed Marouf al-Bakhit as Prime Minister. He was charged with implementing 'true political reforms'. The Islamist opposition spoke out against Bakhit's appointment but have also stated that they have no wish to oust the King.

Economy

Jordan is a small country with limited natural resources but it has been implementing, since 1989, a strong stabilization and structural reform program. The real growth rate of GDP is around 5% (2006 estimate).

Only 10% of its land is fertile, and even that has low and variable rainfall. Its major natural resources are phosphates and potash. Without substantial fossil fuels, apart from natural gas, which supplies 10% of its domestic energy needs, Jordan is dependant on other countries for most of its oil. Tourism is the single largest industry in Jordan, contributing 9–12% of GDP and comes second to workers' remittances from abroad as a source of hard currency earnings.

The political situation in much of the the Middle East has reduced regional trade and development with Iraq, Saudi Arabia, the Gulf states and the West Bank. It has also affected the optimism that followed the peace treaty between Jordan and Israel in 1994.

Below: *The Jordan Valley is the country's most fertile area.*

In 1989, Jordan agreed a five-year plan with the **International Monetary Fund** (IMF) to restore sustainable growth, curb inflation, stabilize the exchange rate and reduce financial imbalances. The strong improvement in the country's economic performance was derailed by the Gulf Crisis of 1990–91. In October 1991, the government concluded a new seven-year economic adjustment program with the IMF. Jordan has now liberalized the trade regime sufficiently to secure membership in the World Trade Organization (WTO), a free trade accord with the **USA**, and an association agreement with the **European Union**. The main challenges still facing Jordan are reducing dependence on foreign grants, reducing the budget deficit and creating investment incentives to promote further job creation.

Above: *Coloured sand bottles where incredibly intricate designs can be created using a funnel and knitting needle.*

THE PEOPLE

The majority of Jordan's 6 million people are Arabs. In addition, there are **Circassians**, and a much smaller group of **Chechens**. Jordan also has a small **Armenian** population.

More than 92% of all Jordanian people are **Sunni Muslims**. The majority of Jordan's **Christians** belong to the **Greek Orthodox** Church, but there are also **Greek Catholics** and a small **Roman Catholic** community, as well as **Syrian Orthodox**, **Coptic Orthodox**, **Armenian Orthodox** and a few **Protestant** denominations. Several small **Shi'a** and **Druze** populations can also be found. The tradition of tolerance and appreciation for diversity is a principle of Hashemite Jordan, which provides a stable social foundation for the country.

BEDOUIN

The Bedouin are nomadic desert-dwellers found throughout Jordan. Traditionally they live in family units within a tribe. Although many have forsaken the old way of life, many families still live in traditional goat's-hair tents. They are a pastoral people and make their living from their sheep and goats. They are famed for their strongly developed codes of honour and hospitality and are the carriers of Jordan's oral tradition of folk music, dance and poetry.

The Bedouins

One of the best known groups from Jordan's population is the Bedouins or 'desert dwellers'. It is difficult to count Bedouins, but it is generally known that the majority of Jordan's population is of Bedouin origin. Most of Jordan's Bedouins live in the vast wasteland that extends east from the **Desert Highway**. Their communities are marked by characteristic black goat's-hair tents. Only a small portion of Bedouins can still be regarded as true **nomads**, while many have settled down to cultivate crops rather than drive their animals across the desert. Many Bedouins have combined the two lifestyles to some degree.

Bedouins are most famous for their **hospitality**, and no traveller is turned away. The values of Bedouin society are vested in an ancient code of honour, calling for total loyalty to the clan and tribe in order to uphold the survival of the group.

The Palestinians

Some Jordanians are of Palestinian origin. There are currently close to 1.4 million Palestinian refugees registered in Jordan. Although massive influxes of refugees have strained Jordan's economy, Palestinian Jordanians have contributed greatly to the health and prosperity of the country.

The Circassians

The Circassians, a non-Arab Islamic people from the Caucasus region of western Asia, first arrived in Jordan in 1878. Estimates of the Circassian population vary from 20,000 to 80,000. Circassian culture places strong emphasis on respect for the elderly and close-knit extended families.

Food and Drink

Jordan's food is essentially Bedouin, mixed with a wide range of foods originating throughout the Middle East. The national dish is known as **mansaf**; this is a whole stewed lamb, cooked in a yoghurt sauce and served on a bed of rice. **Maglouba** is a meat, fish or vegetable stew served with rice, and **musakhan** is a tasty chicken dish, cooked with onions, olive oil and pine seeds. It is baked in the oven on a thick loaf of Arabic bread.

PALESTINIANS

The word 'Palestinian' is derived from the Philistines, who lived in the area in biblical times. In the early 20th century, both Arabs and Jews living in Palestine were known as Palestinians – in fact the Zionist newspaper was known as *The Palestine Post*. Nowadays the term Palestinian is used to describe mainly Islamic Arabs, living in the Palestinian territories, in Jordan or elsewhere, who lived in Palestine before 1948. Many Jordanian citizens are Palestinian refugees.

Opposite: *Jordan Tracks is the only travel agency based in Wadi Rum and is run by local Bedouin.* **Left:** *Meze – a selection of salads, falafel and olives served with dips such as hummus and yoghurt.*

MANSAF

Traditionally this would be served on a large communal platter and eaten using the right hand. The bottom of the dish is layered with *shrak* bread, then covered with rice. On top of this is placed the lamb and a dried yoghurt, called *jameed*, made from goats' milk. Almonds and pine nuts may be used as a garnish and, if it's truly traditional, the sheep's head will then sit on top.

Also popular is the famous Middle Eastern **shish kebab**, consisting of chunks of lamb or marinated chicken speared on a wooden stick and cooked over a charcoal fire with tomatoes and onions. Delicious selections of **meze** are served everywhere – salads, falafel, olives and other titbits are served with hummus, tahini, yoghurt and other dips.

Alcoholic drinks are widely available and the local drink is **arak**, an anise-flavoured drink served with ice and water.

Architecture

The empires which rose and fell over the centuries have left their mark on Jordan's architecture. From antiquity there are Greek remains at Qasr al-Abd and Roman remains everywhere, but notably at Jerash. The classical influence of the Romans can be seen too at Petra, the unique rose-red city of the Nabateans.

The churches of the Byzantine period have left impressive examples of **mosaic artistry**, the greatest of which is undoubtedly the 6th-century **Map of the Holy Land** at Madaba. The Islamic influence is everywhere, from the Desert Castles of the Umayyads to modern mosques like the beautiful **King Abdullah Mosque** in Amman.

Opposite: *A huge jewel-encrusted treasure chest, just one of many fine craft items for sale in a souvenir shop.*
Right: *Details from a mosaic floor within Madaba Museum.*

Crafts

The tradition of crafts in Bedouin culture is closely woven with the way of life. **Embroidery** and **weaving** provided many of the needs and wants of a nomadic way of life. **Horse blankets** and **tents**, **cushions** and **containers** were all woven with naturally dyed wool on a loom pegged to the ground. Clothing, particularly for ceremonial occasions, was richly embroidered with patterns and colours handed down through generations of a family. Many of these traditional craft items are now marketed, providing much-needed employment, particularly in poorer areas. The old traditions have also been incorporated into fashionable new designs and colours.

Jewellery too was part of the Bedouin tradition in that her jewellery was a woman's wealth. Jewellery is still extremely popular in Jordan, and artisans in **silver** and **gold** produce a dazzling variety of pieces for sale in the souks. In workshops in Amman, Madaba and Na'ur, the traditional mouth-blown '**Hebron Glass**', named after the West Bank city, is produced. Originally made from sand, but now from recycled glass, it comes in simple shapes and brilliant colours of cobalt blue, bottle green, turquoise, amber and rose.

King Abdullah II

The current monarch is half English. His mother was born in England, the daughter of a British army officer. Abdullah was educated in Jordan, England and the USA. He subsequently attended Pembroke College, Oxford, and the Royal Military Academy at Sandhurst in the UK. Since his accession Jordan's annual economic growth has doubled and he has been responsible for attracting increased foreign investment and paving the way for the free trade zone at Aqaba.

2
Amman

Amman, Jordan's capital city, is, like Ancient Rome, built on seven hills. It is one of the oldest continually inhabited cities in the world but don't let that fool you. Apart from a few isolated remains it is a product of the 20th century. Modern excavations have revealed homes from the Stone Age some 7000 years before the birth of Christ. Amman is mentioned in the Bible as **Rabbath-Ammon**, the capital of the Ammonites who fought many wars against the Israelites. During one of them the Israeli King, David, had Uriah the Hittite slaughtered here because he coveted his wife.

By the 3rd century BCE the city had been renamed **Philadelphia** after the Ptolemaic ruler Philadelphus. It then passed through Seleucid and Nabatean hands before becoming part of the Decapolis League under the Romans in 30BCE.

After the Romans came the Byzantines, and Philadelphia became the seat of a Christian Bishop. That changed again in 635CE when the advancing armies of Islam took the city and it reverted to its original name.

Amman had always stood at a major crossroads and much of its prosperity was derived from the caravans that passed. Neighbouring **As Salt** then became the trading and administrative centre for the region. Later, when the Ottoman sultans decided to link Damascus to Medina by building the Hejaz railway, Amman was included as a major stop and its fortunes began to improve.

When the **Emirate of Transjordan** was created, after the Great Arab Revolt of World War II, Emir Abdullah

DON'T MISS

*** **The Citadel:** gives the best view of the city.
*** **Roman Theatre:** a perfectly preserved example.
*** **Umayyad Palace:** the most fascinating building in Amman.
** **Hejaz Railway Station:** a wonderful ancient railway.
** **National Archaeological Museum:** this museum puts it all in context.

Opposite: *The columns of the Temple of Hercules at Amman's Citadel can be seen all over the city.*

Above: *Jordanian sign-posts are in English as well as Arabic.*

bin al-Hussein made Amman his capital.

By the close of the 20th century, Amman had grown into the modern capital you see today. Much of the expansion is down to the political situation in the Middle East. The creation of the State of Israel produced waves of Palestinian **refugees** who settled here after being forcibly and illegally evicted from their lands in 1948 and again in 1967. The Gulf War of 1990–91 brought further waves of **immigrants** fleeing from Iraq and Kuwait.

Modern Amman is defined by its seven hills, or *jebels*. Each of these neighbourhoods once had a traffic circle, or roundabout, and directions are given in relation to them. This can be confusing as several of the circles have now been replaced by traffic lights. **First Circle** is near downtown and from there the city spreads westward to **Eighth Circle**.

Amman has a few must-see sights and these can easily be covered in a day or less. But it has much more to offer than antiquities. It's one of the safest and friendliest cities on earth and it is worth spending time just soaking up the atmosphere in its souks and bazaars, modern shopping malls, traditional stores and coffee houses.

THE CITADEL ★★★

Towering above the city on Jebel al-Qal'a is **The Citadel**, site of the ancient city of Rabbath-Ammon. This is the best place to start any tour of Amman, but take a taxi rather than climb the road to the top. Excavations are ongoing on this site and so far archaeologists have uncovered remains from the Roman, Byzantine and Islamic settlements.

The two huge columns that can be seen from all over Amman are part of the **Temple of Hercules** or the

THE DEAD SEA SCROLLS

In 1947 a Bedouin shepherd called **Mohammed Ahmed el-Hamed** discovered some ancient scrolls in a cave near the **Wadi Qumran** on the West Bank of the Jordan River. Subsequent excavations in 11 caves unearthed more scrolls. Written in several forms of ancient Hebrew, they were created some time between the 2nd century BCE and the 1st century CE and are the earliest known biblical documents.

Great Temple of Amman. An inscription shows that it was built between 161 and 166CE during the reign of the emperor Marcus Aurelius by the governor, Germinius Marcianus. Although most of the stone from the temple has been recycled over the centuries, the outline and the restored portico gives you an idea of the sheer scale of the place. It was similar to the **Temple of Artemis** at **Jerash**.

Close by the temple is the small but very important **National Archaeological Museum**. It's a good idea to start your visit here. The collections of pottery, glass, flint and metal tools from around Jordan are arranged in chronological order, and a wander round them will help put the rest of the Citadel in context. Even if you're short of time don't miss the limestone statues from **Ain Ghazal**, an early Neolithic village found near Amman on the banks of the Zarqa River; four rare

THE UMAYYADS

This was the first great Muslim dynasty and ruled the Islamic world from 661–750CE. They came to power following the succession of Ali, son-in-law of Mohammed, as 4th Caliph. Muawiya, governor of Syria, disputed Ali's succession, but Ali was assassinated and Muawiya established the Umayyad Caliphate in Damascus. Under the Umayyads Islamic art and architecture flourished, including the building of the Dome of the Rock on the site of Solomon's Temple in Jerusalem.

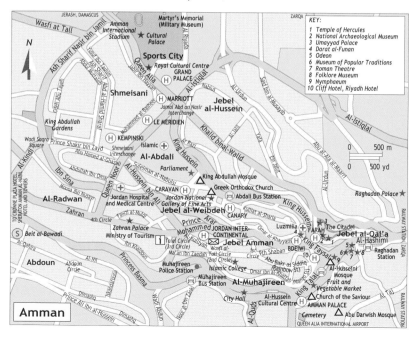

KEY:
1 Temple of Hercules
2 National Archaeological Museum
3 Umayyad Palace
4 Darat al-Funan
5 Odeon
6 Museum of Popular Traditions
7 Roman Theatre
8 Folklore Museum
9 Nymphaeum
10 Cliff Hotel, Riyadh Hotel

sarcophagi from the Iron Age; and a copy of the famous **Mesha Stele** (see panel, page 13) erected by the Moabite King Mesha in 850BCE to celebrate his victories over the Israelites.

The most important display is Jordan's collection of the **Dead Sea Scrolls**, the earliest known biblical texts ever discovered. Found stored in caves on the West Bank of the River Jordan, they were written some time between 50BCE and 68–70CE. One of the scrolls tells of a massive treasure hidden somewhere on the West Bank. So far nothing has been found. Open daily, 08:30–17:00 (09:00–16:00 on Fridays and official holidays).

After the museum walk towards the buildings on the upper terrace. **Al-Qasr**, which translates as **The Palace**, is the centrepiece of what was once a city. Built in the early 8th century by the Umayyads, it offers a unique insight into their approach to architectural planning. Most surviving examples of Umayyad architecture in the Middle East are solitary buildings, making this city unique. Excavations are ongoing but you can explore the extensive city layout and walk along a colonnaded street to the entrance or **Audience Hall**. This massive domed structure may have been the link between the palace and the rest of the city. Islamic architecture started to flourish with the Umayyad Dynasty but they were not above borrowing from previous cultures. The geometric patterns and stucco colonnettes of the decoration inside this building owe much to Sassanid influence, while the layout is Byzantine.

From al-Qasr make your way towards the Corinthian columns which mark the site of a small **Byzantine Church** thought to date from the 6th or 7th centuries CE. This was part of a Byzantine city which stood on this site for several centuries until it was destroyed by the Persian Sassanids.

NEW NATIONAL MUSEUM

A new **Jordan National Museum** is being built in Ras al-Ain near the Al-Hussein Cultural Centre and the City Hall. Work is well under way, with opening planned for May 2011. The three-storey building will have a series of exhibition halls covering history and culture from the earliest times through events such as the Great Arab Revolt to the 21st century. When complete it is likely that many exhibits from the Archaeological Museum, including the Dead Sea Scrolls, will move here.

DOWNTOWN ★★★

Most of Roman Philadelphia can be seen from the Citadel but for a closer look head downhill and along **Al-Hashimi Street**.

The Forum, Philadelphia's original market place, was at the very heart of the city. All that remains now is some of the original paving and a long Corinthian colonnade.

The largest of the remains are just beyond the forum. The massive **Roman Theatre** was built during the reign of Antonius Pius (138–161CE). It was cut into the side of a hill and is similar in design to the theatre at Jerash. It is still used as a major venue for concerts and can seat 6000 people. Open Wednesday–Monday, 09:00–16:00.

Two small but very worthwhile museums can be accessed from either end of the Roman stage. On the left the **Museum of Popular Traditions** houses some of the 6th-century mosaics from the cities of **Jerash** and **Madaba** as well as collections of antique jewellery and displays of traditional costumes. A statue of a Bedouin of the Desert Patrol guards the entrance. The museums are open Saturday–Thursday, 09:00–17:00 and Friday, 09:00–16:00.

At the other end the **Folklore Museum** deals with the traditional way of life of local people. The statue guarding

---

GLUBB PASHA

Sir John Bagot Glubb was a British soldier attached to the army of Transjordan. As an officer in the Arab Legion he was responsible for forming the Desert Patrol. In 1939 he assumed command of the Legion and transformed it into the finest fighting force in the Arab world. In 1948 they occupied the West Bank, and Glubb remained in charge of defences there until he was dismissed by King Hussein in 1956.

Opposite: *The gigantic hand from a statue of Hercules is displayed outside the National Archaeological Museum.* **Below:** *The finest view of Amman's Roman Theatre is from the Temple of Hercules at the Citadel.*

AL-PASHA TURKISH BATH

Although built in the traditional Ottoman style, this is a modern 20th-century *hammam*. It's in Mahmoud Taha Street and opens from 10:00 until midnight. For a mere 15JD you can spend two hours here enjoying the sauna and steam rooms, having your skin soaped and scrubbed, then massaged with olive oil. There are women- and men-only sessions and by pre-booking they can accommodate couples or mixed groups.

Below: *The King Abdullah Mosque, built in the 1980s, is a superb example of modern Islamic architecture.*

the entrance here is of a Circassian in traditional dress. A Bedouin tent is at the centre of a tableau depicting desert life, while an accurately recreated living room from an Ammani house shows how different was the life of city dwellers. Another exhibit covers the process of traditional rug weaving and there are collections of guns, agricultural tools and musical instruments. Open Saturday–Thursday, 08:00–20:00 and Friday, 09:00–16:00.

Just along from the Folklore Museum is the **Odeon**, a small Roman theatre of some 500 seats which was completely renovated by 1997. It dates from the early 2nd century CE and was probably a venue for music concerts as it is now. Like the large theatre it is open air but archaeologists think that it may have had a temporary wooden or tent-like roof to shelter audiences.

Go back through the forum and turn left onto Al-Hashimi Street. Keep left when the road forks to reach the **Nymphaeum**.

This was the city's main fountain, built in 191CE. It was an enormous structure containing a 600m (656yd) square pool with water 3m (10ft) deep. It's similar in size and design to the Nymphaeum at Jerash. These

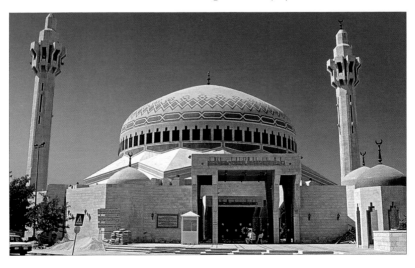

fountains were common in ancient Roman cities. They were usually built next to a source of running water and dedicated to water nymphs. Amman's Nymphaeum is currently being excavated and should be restored to its original splendour by 2010.

A short stroll from the Nymphaeum will bring you to **Al-Husseini Mosque**, not to be confused with the new King Hussein Mosque in the Dabouq suburb, behind King Hussein Gardens. This one was built in pink and white stone in the Ottoman style by the late King Abdullah I in 1924 and restored in 1987. It was constructed on the site of a much older mosque, probably erected around 640CE by the 2nd Caliph of Islam, Omar ibn Al-Khattab. Archaeologists believe that this may also have been the site of Philadelphia's Byzantine Cathedral.

Above: *A typical street in Amman will have lots of interesting and quirky shops to explore.*

The oldest road in Amman, **King Faysal Street**, heads away from the mosque. Along here, near where the street forks, is the famous gold souk. Over 50 shops are crammed into this space, selling everything imaginable, from bracelets and earrings to necklaces and gold coffee pots.

West Amman **

Darat Al-Funun, the Little House of the Arts, is a short but steep climb up Omar al-Khayyam Street. Set in a tranquil garden away from the bustle of the city, this is the place to come and find out about contemporary Arab art. It also has several historic connections. Of the three 1920s villas on this site, the main building was once the home of Peak Pasha – Captain, later, Lieutenant Colonel Frederick Peak – who commanded the Arab Legion from the early 1920s until 1939. Now restored by the artist and architect, Ammar Khammash, it is the main gallery housing works by leading Arab artists. Open Saturday–Thursday, 10:00–19:00; during Ramadan, 10:00–15:00.

GOLD

Gold is sold by weight irrespective of the quality of the workmanship. Incredible bargains can usually be found in the Gold Souk. As Jordanian gold does not have hallmarks, its quality has to be determined from a stamp showing gold purity. This is in parts per thousand, with '750' and '875' indicating 18 and 21 carat. The up-market shops of Shmeisani and Sweifiyyeh are where to find the more expensive 18 carat gold and white gold.

Below: *Jordan's Martyr's
Memorial is a tribute to
Jordanian soldiers who
gave their lives in service
of their country.*

Jordan National Gallery of Fine Arts **

The Royal Society for Fine Arts established this gallery
in a town house at Jebel al-Weibdeh. It contains a
selection of the best in contemporary art, both from
Jordanian artists and from others elsewhere in the
Islamic world. Open Saturday–Monday, Wednesday
and Thursday, 09:00–19:00 (closes at 17:00 in winter
and 15:30 during Ramadan). Closed on Eid al-Fitr, Eid
al-Adha, Christmas and New Year's Day.

King Abdullah Mosque **

Built between 1982 and 1989 as a memorial to the
assassinated King Abdullah I, this is one of the grandest
mosques built in the Middle East in modern times.
Capped by a huge blue mosaic dome, surrounded by
eight smaller domes and flanked by two minarets, it is a
striking landmark. Up to 3000 worshippers at a time
can be accommodated for prayer.

Martyr's Memorial *

This large memorial of white stone houses Jordan's
Military Museum. Its displays and collections cover all
of Jordan's armed conflicts from the Great Arab Revolt
of World War I up to the present day. Outside the building is part of Jordan's collection of military vehicles. It is
located at **Sports City** in the **Shmeisani** area of Amman.
Open Saturday–Thursday, 09:00–16:00.

Left: *Abu Darwish, also known as Hasan Mustafa Sharkas, was the Circasian immigrant who built this unusual mosque in 1961.*

Abu Darwish Mosque **

This rather unusual mosque on top of **Jebel al-Ashrafiyeh** is unique in Jordan because of its covering of black and white stone in a chequered pattern. It was built in 1961 by a Circasian immigrant, Hasan Mustafa Sharkas, who was also known as Abu Darwish. Look out for the decorations around the walls. They look like chess pawns.

Royal Automobile Museum **

Set in **Al-Hussein National Park**, the largest park in the capital, the building is an unusual design by the architect Jafar Tukan. He visualized it as complementing the natural landscape and had it substantially submerged in the ground and clad in natural untreated stone.

But it is the fantastic collection of cars and motorbikes that is the highlight of any visit. From the 1916 type 53 Cadillac, similar to the one which Sharrif Hussein used for his return to Jordan, to the 1993 Porsche that King Hussein used when in England, the vehicles offer a different look at the history of the Kingdom.

The late King Hussein had a passion for automobiles and most of the cars were owned or used by him. There are the 1952 Lincoln Capri he used while a student in England and the 1955 Mercedes 300SL 'Gullwing' that he raced at Jordan's Rumman Hill Climb. Open Wednesday–Monday, 10:00–19:00 (Friday open from 11:00).

JOHN THE BAPTIST

John was a Jewish preacher from the 1st century CE. According to the Gospel of Luke he was a relative of Jesus. He is regarded as a prophet by Christianity, Islam and the Bahá'í faith. Christians call him the Baptist because of his practice of baptizing people in the River Jordan. About six months after he baptized Jesus, John was imprisoned by Herod Antipas in his fortress at Machaerus and subsequently beheaded.

Right: *The stationmaster of the Hejaz Railway in Jordan demonstrates a model train in the Railway Museum.*

Hejaz Railway Station ★★★

Whether or not you're a railway buff, this is one Amman attraction not to be missed. Walking through the arched gateway into **Al Mahata**, Amman's railway station, is like stepping through a portal into a bygone age. Travel on this railway is spasmodic at best and reports of recent activity often turn out to be false, so check with the station before contemplating any journey. In June 2010 the *Jordanian Times* ran a story of a regular Saturday excursion to Syria.

There is a splendid little **museum** attached to the station. It does not appear to have regular opening hours but the very friendly Station Master may be prepared to let you in on request.

Cave of Seven Sleepers ★

There's a legend about seven young Christian men who hid in this quadruple chambered cave to escape persecution by the Romans. The **Qur'an**, Sura 18, describes how they were threatened with death if they refused to worship a pagan Roman god. Taking refuge in the cave they fell asleep for a period of between 10

HEJAZ RAILWAY

The Ottomans built this line in 1900 to link Damascus with the holy city of Mecca. However, the outbreak of World War I meant that it stopped at Medina. During the Arab Revolt the line came under attack from forces led by Lawrence of Arabia. The section from the Saudi border to Medina has been closed since. South of Amman only a small section of track is in use to ferry phosphates from the mines near Ma'an.

and 30 years. When they awoke they went to buy food using their, by now, ancient money. The shopkeeper took them to the governor, who was a Christian, and he ordered celebrations. Thereafter the boys returned to the cave where they fell into a permanent sleep. Situated 4km (2.5 miles) south of Downtown in the suburb of Abu Alanda next to the green domed mosque of Ahl el-Kahf, the cave is open daily, 08:00–17:00.

As Salt *

This long-established agricultural town, located 29km (18 miles) northwest of Amman, was a regional capital at the time of the Ottomans and by the 19th century had eclipsed Amman as the main trading centre. However, the construction of the Hejaz Railway and Emir Abdullah's choice of Amman as capital of Trans-jordan swung the pendulum in the opposite direction.

One of the best reasons for visiting As Salt today is to see the fabulous examples of Ottoman architecture. The houses climb the sides of three small hills and the best way to view them is simply to stroll around the streets. The main attraction is **Salt Cultural Centre**, just off Maydan Street. There's a small museum in the centre with displays showing examples of traditional life including weaving, milking sheep and grinding coffee. Open daily, 08:00–19:00.

Salt Traditional Crafts Centre is also on Maydan Street and has workshops producing textile prints, ceramics and weaving. You can also buy some of these products in the shop. Open daily, 08:00–19:00.

> **ELIJAH**
>
> Elijah was an Old Testament prophet who lived in the 8th and 9th centuries BCE and was famed for bringing the dead back to life and foretelling doom and disaster to non-believers. He appears in both the Hebrew and Christian Bibles and the Qur'an and is one of only two biblical characters who did not die. According to the *Book of Kings* Elijah ascended to heaven in a chariot of fire.

Below: *The fabulous Ottoman houses in As Salt climb up the sides of the surrounding hills.*

Amman at a Glance

Spring (March–May) and autumn (September–October) are the best times to visit. The days are temperate at around 19–30°C (66–86°F). Most of the rain in Jordan falls in the winter months. The nights are chilly year-round. In summer the days are extremely hot, while in winter days and nights are cold.

This is the main point of arrival in Jordan for most visitors. Queen Alia International Airport lies 35km (22 miles) south of Amman. Airport Express buses provide onward transport to Amman's Abdali bus station via the Shmeisiani area. Taxis are plentiful but go to the airport taxi office in the arrivals area and they will issue a slip showing the correct fixed price for the trip to Amman. If you take a taxi without getting this slip you will be overcharged.

Driving in Amman can be a challenge, mainly due to poor or non-existent signposting. The best and cheapest way to get about the capital is to use the yellow private taxis. Hail them on the street. They are metered and inexpensive. The taxis on the ranks outside the large hotels, on the other hand, probably won't use their meters and will charge over the odds. For travel outside of Amman

hiring a car is the best option. The big international companies all have a presence in Amman but often the best deals are with local companies. **Rent a Reliable Car** provides a first-class service: 19 Fawzi Al-Qaweqji Street, PO Box 960643, Amman 11196, tel: 06 592 9676, www.reliable.com

LUXURY
Crowne Plaza Hotel, King Faysal Bin Abdul Azia Street, Amman, 950555, tel: 06 551 0001, www.cpamman.com Thirty minutes' drive from Queen Alia International Airport and situated right in the heart of the city centre.
Holiday Inn, Madina Al-Munawarah Street, PO Box 941825, Amman, 11194, tel: 06 552 8822, www.holiday inn.com In western Amman, close to the main shopping centres and just 30 minutes' drive from the airport.
Kempinski, Abdul Hameed Shouman Street, Shmeisani, PO Box 941045, Amman, 11194, tel: 06 520 0200, www.kempinski-amman.com Unashamed luxury with fine dining and splendid views. One of the best hotels in the city centre.
Le Meridien, Queen Noor Street, Shmeisani, PO Box 950629, Amman, 11195, tel: 06 569 6511, www.starwood hotels.com/lemeridien/ property/overview/index.

html?propertyID=1878 Another world-class hotel in the heart of the city, with a choice of international cuisine including food from Lebanon, Japan and Mongolia.
Marriott, Shmeissani Issam Ajluni Street, PO Box 926333, Amman, 11190, tel: 06 560 7607, www. marriott.co.uk/hotels/travel/ ammjr-amman-marriott-hotel/ Centrally located in the Shmeisani area, this hotel is ideal for both business and leisure travellers, being close to tourist attractions, shopping and also the business district.
Sheraton Amman Al-Nabil Hotel & Towers, 5th Circle, PO Box 840064, Amman, 11184, tel: 06 593 4111, www.starwoodhotels.com/ sheraton/property/overview/ index.html?propertyID=1239 This magnificent white stone building is on a hilltop site in the heart of Amman's embassy and business district.

MID-RANGE
Caravan Hotel, Suleiman al-Nabulsi Street, Jebel al-Weibdeh, Amman, 11191, tel: 06 566 1195. Very handy for the bus terminal and the King Abdullah Mosque. Both this excellent hostel and its sister establishment, The Canary, are run by the Al-Twal family who also operate the superb Mariam Hotel in Madaba.

Amman at a Glance

The Canary Hotel, Al-Karmali Street, Jebel al-Weibdeh, Amman, 11191, tel: 06 463 8353. Near the city centre and the bus terminal. Superb small budget hotel run by a family who know the meaning of hospitality.

BUDGET
Bdeiwi Hotel, Omar al-Khayyam Street, Amman, tel: 06 464 3394, www.hostels. com/hostels/amman/bdeiwi-hostel&hotel/32796 This is on a street behind and uphill from the post office. Cheap, cheerful and clean with a friendly proprietor, ceiling fans and free hot showers.
The Cliff Hotel, between Prince Mohammed Street and Basman Street (in an alley opposite Hashem's Restaurant), tel: 06 462 4273. A bit difficult to find but well worth the effort. Probably Amman's favourite backpacker hotel.
Farah Hotel, Al-Hussein Cinema Street (behind the downtown Arab Bank), tel: 06 465 1443, www.hostels. com/hostels/amman/farah-hotel/8764 Cheap and cheerful hostel accommodation comprising single and double rooms and four-bed dormitories. One of the most popular backpacker hotels in Amman.
Palace Hotel, King Faysal Street, Amman, tel: 06 462 4327, www.hostels.com/ hostels/amman/palace-hotel/ 12022 The Palace is near the Gold Souk and within easy

access of the Roman remains and the Citadel. Choice of rooms with shared bathrooms or the deluxe with *en-suite* bathroom and air conditioning.
Riyadh Hotel, Off King Faysal St (located in an alley off the street), tel: 06 462 4260. Cheap and clean with ceiling fans and friendly staff. Well situated for exploring downtown.

WHERE TO EAT

Al Mukhtar, Le Meridien Hotel, tel: 06 569 6511. Arab cuisine produced to the high standards of Le Meridien.
Fakhereddin, 1st Circle (behind the Iraqi Embassy on Taha Hussein Street), tel: 06 465 2399. One of the finest restaurants in the capital. Not cheap but well worth the money. Reservations are essential.
Hashem, opposite the Cliff Hotel, tel: 06 463 6440. Long established cheap and cheerful diner with limited menu. Tables set out in an alleyway. Possibly one of the cheapest places to eat in Amman.
Tannoureen, Shatt al-Arab Street (near 6th Circle), tel: 06 551 5987. Although expensive, the superb

Lebanese food, a huge menu and first-class service make this one not to be missed.

TOURS AND EXCURSIONS

Jordan Circle Tours, Jebel Amman, Al-Hayyek Street (opposite Housing Bank), Amman, tel: 06 464 3017, www.jct.com.jo
Abercrombie & Kent Jordan, Abdullah Bin Abbas Street (opposite Orchid's Hotel), Amman, tel: 06 566 5465, www.akdmc.com
Al-Thuraya Travel & Tours, PO Box 1883, Amman 11821, tel: 06 553 5525, www.althurayatravel.net
Jordan Tracks, PO Box 468, Aqaba, tel: 7964 82801, www.jordantracks.com
Saleem Ali and his family operate the only Bedouin-owned tourist agency in Jordan, based in Wadi Rum. They also organize tours and excursions throughout Jordan.

USEFUL CONTACTS

Emergency calls, tel: 196.
British Embassy, tel: 06 590 9200.
US Embassy, tel: 06 590 6000.
Al-Khalidi Medical Centre, tel: 06 464 4281.

AMMAN	J	F	M	A	M	J	J	A	S	O	N	D
AVERAGE TEMP. °F	55	57	66	73	82	86	91	91	86	79	68	59
AVERAGE TEMP. °C	13	14	19	23	28	30	33	33	30	26	20	15
RAINFALL in	2.4	2.8	1.4	3.6	0.8	0	0	0	0	0.8	0.4	2
RAINFALL mm	60	70	35	9	2	0	0	0	0	2	10	50
DAYS OF RAINFALL	5	6	3	1	1	0	0	0	0	1	1	4

3
North of Amman & the Jordan Valley

The area to the north of Amman is the most densely populated part of the country. The Jordan Valley is part of the well-known **Great Rift Valley** – a geological fault which runs from Syria to Mozambique and also connects **Lake Tiberias** (the Sea of Galilee) to the **Dead Sea**. The River Jordan, which runs between these two bodies of water, forms Jordan's border with **Israel**, although it now bears very little resemblance to the majestic river of the Bible. Extensive irrigation on both banks has reduced it to a mere trickle a few metres wide. But this irrigation, combined with the temperatures of the lowest cultivated land on earth, enables local farmers to have their fruit and vegetables ripening weeks before other areas.

It's an incredibly fertile area of olive and fig groves, lush vegetation, rolling hills and some of the finest **antiquities** in the Middle East. Here you will find Crusader and Saracen castles, Byzantine art and architecture, and ancient settlements from the Bronze Age to Roman times.

To travel in Jordan is to journey through both the Old and the New Testament. In fact, the **Bible** could be described as the original guidebook to the country. A hire car or taxi is the best way to get about but make sure you have your passport with you at all times because there are frequent military checkpoints. When approaching one, slow down, open your window, smile and speak in English. On most occasions you will just be waved through.

DON'T MISS

*** Jerash: one of the best-preserved Roman cities in the Middle East.
*** Chariot racing: 21st-century chariot racing at Jerash Hippodrome.
*** Umm Qais: Jesus walked through this atmospheric ruined city.
** Ajloun: Saladin's stronghold expanded by the Mamelukes.
** Pella: fantastic view from the terrace of the rest house.
* Abila: painted tombs cut into the hillside during the Roman occupation.

Opposite: *Jerash, Jordan's best-preserved Roman city, is impressive.*

Below: *Hadrian's Arch was built in honour of the Roman Emperor who visited Jerash in 129CE.*

Jerash ★★★

Often called the 'Pompeii of the East', Jerash is one of the largest and finest of the ancient **Roman** cities to be found outside of Italy, and rivaled only by **Ephesus** in Turkey.

People have lived in this fertile, well-watered area for more than six and a half thousand years. The early inhabitants of the first millenia BCE called it Gashu. Later this was Hellenized to Gerasa, then Arab and Circasian settlers changed it to Jerash.

Gashu was little more than a village until the 2nd century BCE, when the forces of **Alexander the Great** started constructing the city whose remains you see today. But its golden age dates from its inclusion, by the Emperor Pompey, in the **Roman Decapolis League** in 63BCE. It was during the Roman occupation that the main city plan of a colonnaded main street intersected by side streets was laid out.

Jerash flourished through trade with the **Nabateans**. When the **Emperor Trajan** annexed the Nabatean kingdom and built the **Via Nova Traiana** (Trajan New Road) from Syria to **Aqaba**, even greater wealth was generated. This was used to erect great buildings using granite from Aswan in Egypt. When the **Emperor Hadrian** visited in 129CE the city built the massive **Hadrian's Arch** in his honour. After obtaining tickets from the office you enter the city through this triumphal arch. A day or more can easily be devoted to Jerash but if time is tight a couple of hours' walking will cover most of the highlights.

Just past the arch is the newly restored **Hippodrome**. Nearly 15,000 people could be seated here to watch the sports and chariot

races. Continuing along the path you come to the **City Walls** built in the early 4th century by the **Emperor Diocletian**. Pass through the **South Gate** to enter the city proper and continue to the **Oval Plaza**. This spectacular paved area with its altars and 7th-century fountain is surrounded by colonnades of 1st-century Ionic columns. From here the **Cardo Maximus**, or main colonnaded street, forms the backbone of the city. Its Ionic columns were replaced with rather more elaborate Corinthian ones during the 2nd century. Shops once lined both sides of this elegant boulevard and a state of the art (for the time) underground sewage and rainwater system ran its full length.

Halfway along the street is the **Macellum**, or marketplace, on the left, then the **South Tetrapylon** – the first of two cross streets. This is marked by four columns although only their pedestals can still be seen.

Next along on the left is a building known as the **Cathedral** – a Byzantine church constructed from the 2nd-century **Temple of Dionysus**. The monumental gateway of that temple is on display and beside it is all that remains of the **Nymphaeum** or public fountain. It's remarkably well preserved and not difficult to imagine what it must have been like when new. It would have had marble facings on the bottom, painted plaster on the upper level and a half-dome roof on top.

Above: *South Theatre, Jerash. The Jordanian Pipe Band is a legacy from the days of the British Army.*

Continuing along the Cardo leads to the next cross street, or North Tetrapylon. Turn left through the massive four-arched entrance that would once have had a domed roof. This was dedicated to the wife of **Emperor Septimus Severus**, Julia Domna. This street, the **North Decumanus**, leads to the 1600-seat **North Theatre**. Beyond the theatre a path to the left leads to the **Temple of Artemis** whose Corinthian columns stand tall on their hilltop site. Continuing on the path leads to the **South Decumanus** and beyond it eventually to the massive **South Theatre**. This is much older than the North Theatre and can seat 3000 people. The acoustics are superb. Standing at the centre of the orchestra floor a speaker can be heard by the entire auditorium. Try it out. Climb to the top seats and get a friend below to speak or sing. The view from the top is also excellent.

You are now back at the Oval Plaza and from there can return to the Cardo. If you have time turn left along it and find the **Museum** building on your right. Many of the artefacts uncovered during various excavations are on display and include examples of coins, jewellery, pottery, glass and gold.

Jerash went into decline from the 3rd century CE when shipping started to replace overland caravans, but it was a series of earthquakes in 747CE that finished it as a great city. Although people still lived here until around 800CE its population had shrunk to some 4000 and it was little more than a rural settlement. Thereafter it disappeared, buried in the sands until it was rediscovered in 1806. Archaeologists started digging in 1925 and the excavations continue. Open daily, 08:00–16:00 (until 19:00 in summer).

CHARIOT RACING

This was a particularly popular sport with the ancient Romans and following the restoration of the Hippodrome at Jerash these spectacular races are once again taking place there. The **Roman Army Chariot Experience** (website: www.jerashchariots.com) stage races and gladiatorial contests twice every day, and once on Fridays. Spectators of the 21st century sit in the same stone seats occupied by the citizens of Jerash over two thousand years earlier.

Ajloun ★★

The busy market town of Ajloun is about 25km (16 miles) west of Jerash. There's a fascinating early 14th-century mosque with carved inscriptions from the Qur'an near the centre. But Ajloun's main attraction is the **Qala'at al-Rabadh** (**Ajloun Castle**). Towering high above the town, this splendid example of medieval Islamic military architecture was built in the early 12th century CE by Azz ad-Din Usama, an Arab general and nephew of the famed Muslim commander **Salah al-Din** (Saladin).

From this fortress the Muslim army commanded the Jordan Valley and three small valleys leading to it. The **Crusaders** made repeated attempts to capture it but were unsuccessful. From a viewpoint high on the castle you can see why. On a clear day you can see south as far as the **Dead Sea**, west across the Jordan Valley to the **West Bank**, and north to the Sea of Galilee. The original castle had just four towers and a wide moat. It was destroyed by Mongol invaders and rebuilt by the **Mamelukes**. Extra towers were added and the castle became a staging post in a beacon network enabling messages to be transmitted from Baghdad to Cairo in a mere 12 hours. Open daily, 09:00–17:00.

MAMELUKES

The Mamelukes were slaves who served as soldiers for the Muslim caliphs and Ayyubid sultans. Mostly they were Circassians and Caucasians who converted to Islam. They are first recorded as serving the Abbasid Dynasty in Baghdad in the 9th century CE. Through time they became a powerful military force and eventually seized power in Egypt in 1250. The Sultanate they established, although a bloody one, survived until it was conquered by the Ottomans in 1517.

Below: *Vaulted chambers in Qala'at al-Rabadh (Ajloun Castle) now accommodate a small museum.*

Pella ★★

Set within a series of hills just beyond the town of
Al-Mashari, the city of **Tabaqat Fahl** is one of the oldest
in Jordan. Continually occupied from Neolithic times,
it may even have been inhabited as far back as the
Palaeolithic period, some 100,000 years ago. Unlike
Jerash only a small part of the site has been excavated
but its location makes it worthy of a visit. Start your
visit at the rest house that sits on a hill overlooking the
site. There on the terrace, with a glass of hot sweet tea,
you can get a marvellous overview of the layout before
heading downhill to wander round the ruins.

Tabaqat Fahl was an important trade centre, linking
Cyprus, Syria and Egypt, from the 19th century BCE.
When the Greeks came they changed its name to Pella,
possibly in honour of the birthplace of Alexander
the Great. Following Pompey's conquest in 63BCE it
became part of the **Roman Decapolis** and enjoyed an
increase in trade and prosperity. One of the earliest
Christian churches was built here by Christians fleeing
from nearby **Jerusalem** during the **Great Jewish Revolt**
of 66CE. During the 5th and 6th centuries, under
Byzantine rule, this prosperity continued, but by the 7th
century decline had set in.

Following the Arab conquest in the 7th century it
became an Umayyad city, until it was destroyed by an
earthquake in 749CE.

Most of the excavated remains are from the Graeco-
Roman period but you can also see what's left of the
walls from the Bronze and Iron ages, the Islamic resid-
ential quarter and a medieval mosque.

Umm Qais ★★★

The modern town of **Umm Qais** doesn't warrant a detour
but on the outskirts are the remains of the **Decapolis** city
of **Gadara**. This is an atmospheric place. Come here
early in the day and climb to the café in the rest room
near the top of the site. Order a cup of mint tea and sit
on the terrace while you get your bearings. From here
you can see all the way along the stone-flagged street of

the Roman city. To your right is the border with Syria, the **Yarmouk valley**, and beyond that the **Golan Heights** and the waters of **Lake Tiberias (the Sea of Galilee)**.

The **West Theatre** was constructed of black basalt in the 2nd century CE and capable of seating 3000 people. Climb to the top row of seats and get another fine view of the Sea of Galilee. Beyond the Theatre, **Church Terrace**

has the remains of a 6th-century square church, which had an octagonal interior and a three-aisled **Basilica**. Underneath the barrel-vaulted roofs of the **Street of Shops** provided the support.

The **Decumanus Maximus**, or Main Street, is a 1.7km (1-mile) preserved section of paved road showing the deep grooves cut into the stone, 2 millennia ago, by chariot wheels. It runs east to west just north of **Church Terrace** and can be reached by heading down the steps from the café. On the right is all that remains of the **Nymphaeum**, a late 2nd-century CE public fountain with a monumental façade inscribed with the names of the Gadarene family who paid for it. A bit further along on the left the overgrown 4th-century **Byzantine Baths**

Above: *Looking out over the remains of a 6th-century square church with octagonal interior towards the Golan Heights in the distance.*

sit behind a fence. A large stretch of the street is colonnaded and it's well worth walking its entire length. A **monumental gateway** marks its end and just before that lie the remains of the **Hippodrome**, once the venue of chariot races. You'll also come across remains from Jordan's more recent

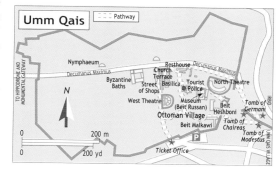

Above: *The view from the terrace café at Umm Qais. The Yarmouk Valley below is the border with Syria. Beyond that is the Golan Heights and the waters of Lake Tiberias (the Sea of Galilee).*

turbulent past. Deserted gun emplacements and lookout stations line this strategic high ground overlooking the border.

This site was occupied as early as the 7th century BCE but most of the visible remains are Roman. From the time it was taken by Pompey in 63BCE and incorporated into the Decapolis it enjoyed centuries of prosperity. It peaked around the 2nd century CE and by then it would have been one of the foremost cities of the country, with colonnaded streets, theatres, baths, temples, shops and houses. An earthquake all but destroyed it in 747CE and from then it was practically deserted. Open daily, 07:00 to sunset.

Irbid *

This city may have been inhabited since the Bronze Age but most of its heritage now lies under the modern, mainly industrial, city that has become the administrative centre for the north of Jordan.

It's an excellent place to visit if you want to see ordinary people going about their lives untrammeled by tourism. Turn off the main street and it's like stepping back in time. Get there early in the morning and watch the local butchers set up shop. A neatly severed cow's head is hung from a hook outside the door with other parts of the carcass swinging alongside. A few worried looking sheep and goats are in a pen nearby. This could be any European city 200 years ago.

At the **Institute of Archaeology and Anthropology** of the Yarmouk University you'll find the **Museum of Jordanian Heritage**, probably the finest archaeological museum in the country. Open daily (except Tuesday), 10:00–17:00 (until 15:00 in winter).

DEIR ALLAH

Literally translated this means 'the House of God'. Today it is a small village surrounded by a farming community in the fertile Jordan Valley. Excavations in the area confirm that people have lived here from 1600BCE and clay tablets recovered from the site are inscribed with a system of writing similar to Phoenician. According to the Bible it was here that Jacob allegedly wrestled with an angel and where he was supposedly reunited with Esau.

Heading out of town on the main road to **Mafraq** you will pass an impressive **monument** on the right-hand side of the road. Built in 2003 in honour of the dead from the 1973 war between **Israel**, **Jordan** and **Syria**, it has an impressive display of old tanks, military vehicles and a British Hawker Hunter Jet. Don't just head up the steps, for although it may look deserted, it is continually manned by the army. Go to the right-hand side of the steps and look for the small office. You will need to tell them you

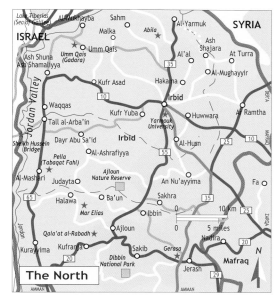

want to have a look, show them your passport and sign the visitor's book.

Abila *

A few kilometres north of Irbid in Wadi Qwayllbey is the **Decapolis City** of Abila. Evidence has been uncovered showing that people lived here from the Bronze Age to the Byzantine period. In 1889 the site was described as having ruins 'of very considerable extent, and show the remains of buildings that must have boasted originally no inconsiderable architectural splendor.' Two mounds created by the remains of nearly ten millennia of human habitation are being painstakingly excavated, so don't expect anything similar to Jerash. But the painted tombs cut into the hill-side of the Roman-era cemetery are well worth a visit. You'll need a car to get there, a drive of 20 minutes north of Irbid. Take food and plenty of water with you as there are no facilities whatsoever.

GOLAN HEIGHTS

This strategic plateau sits on the border of Syria, Lebanon, Jordan and Israel. Although part of Syria, it was captured by the Israelis during the Six Day War. In 1981 Israel passed the Golan Heights Law in order to subject the area to their 'laws, juris-diction and administration'. The United Nations, how-ever, regards the Israeli occu-pation as illegal and has called on them to withdraw.

North of Amman and the Jordan Valley at a Glance

BEST TIMES TO VISIT

Spring (March–May) and autumn (September–October) are the best times to visit. The days are temperate at around 19–30°C (66–86°F). Most of the rain in Jordan falls in the winter months. The nights are chilly year-round. In summer the days are extremely hot, while in winter the days and the nights are cold.

GETTING THERE

Because of a lack of quality hotels, most people tour this area from a base in Amman. It is possible to do a circuit of the main attractions in a day.

GETTING AROUND

All of the towns in northern Jordan are linked by bus, even some of the villages, but this form of transport will limit what you can see unless you have unlimited time. Most of the minibus services only leave when they are full, making planning difficult. Organized tours from Amman will take in the main sites of Jerash, Ajloun and Umm Qais, or else a taxi and driver can be hired by the day to tour the area. Most hotels will be able to organize tours and excursions or make the appropriate recommendations. By far the best option is to rent a self-drive car and explore at your leisure.
Rent a Reliable Car is an excellent local company based in Amman. You can

contact them at 19 Fawzi Al-Qaweqji Street, PO Box 960643, Amman 11196, tel: 06 592 9676.

WHERE TO STAY

Amman
LUXURY
Crowne Plaza Hotel, King Faysal Bin Abdul Azia Street, Amman, 950555, tel: 06 551 0001, www.cpamman.com Thirty minutes' drive from Queen Alia International Airport and situated right in the heart of the city centre.
Holiday Inn, Madina Al-Munawarah Street, PO Box 941825, Amman, 11194, tel: 06 552 8822, www.holiday inn.com In western Amman, close to the main shopping centres and just 30 minutes' drive from the airport.
Kempinski, Abdul Hameed Shouman Street, Shmeisani, PO Box 941045, Amman, 11194, tel: 06 520 0200, www.kempinski-amman.com Unashamed luxury with fine dining and splendid views. One of the best hotels in the city centre.
Le Meridien, Queen Noor Street, Shmeisani, PO Box 950629, Amman, 11195, tel: 06 569 6511, www.starwood hotels.com/lemeridien/property/overview/index.html?propertyID=1878 Another world-class hotel in the heart of the city, with a choice of international cuisine including food from Lebanon, Japan and Mongolia.

Marriott, Shmeissani Issam Ajluni Street, PO Box 926333, Amman, 11190, tel: 06 560 7607, www.marriott.co.uk/hotels/travel/ammjr-amman-marriott-hotel/ Centrally located in the Shmeisani area, this is ideal for both business and leisure travellers, being close to tourist attractions, shopping and the business district.
Sheraton Amman Al-Nabil Hotel & Towers, 5th Circle, PO Box 840064, Amman, 11184, tel: 06 593 4111, www.starwoodhotels.com/sheraton/property/overview/index.html?propertyID=1239 This magnificent white stone building is on a hilltop site in the heart of Amman's embassy and business district.

Ajloun
BUDGET
Ajloun Woodland Reserve Campsite, open March to November and booked via: Royal Society for the Conservation of Nature, PO Box 1215, Amman 11941, tel: 06 533 7931, www.rscn.org.jo The Ajloun Campsite has a series of four-bed tented lodges with shared facilities. It is set within the RSCN Reserve in a grassy clearing enclosed by oak, pistachio and strawberry trees.

Jerash
BUDGET
Olive Branch, PO Box 2314, Amman 11181, tel: 02 634

0555, www.olivebranch.
com.jo This is the nearest
hotel to Jerash and sits in the
hills about 7km (4 miles)
north of the ruins. It is a good
base for exploring all of north
Jordan including Ajloun, Pella
and Umm Qais.

Pella
BUDGET
The Countryside Hotel,
Tabqat Fahl, tel: 07 9557
4145. This small hotel is the
only accommodation option
in the area. It's a few minutes'
drive from the ruins at Pella
and is owned by the manager
of the Pella Rest House. The
facilities are basic but clean.
It was recently redecorated
with a self-catering kitchen
and offers superb views of
the surrounding countryside.

Irbid
MID-RANGE
Al-Joude Hotel, Manama
Street, opposite the University
Mosque on University Street,
tel: 02 727 5515. Three-star
hotel. All the rooms are *en
suite* and have satellite
television.

BUDGET
Abu Baker Hotel, off Orouba
Street, tel: 02 724 2695.
Clean, cheerful, ridiculously
cheap. Showers are free.
Amin Hotel, Orouba Street,
tel: 02 724 2384. Very cheap,
basic accommodation that is
clean and well looked after.
Showers cost a little extra.

Omayed Hotel, Baghdad
Street above the supermarket,
tel: 02 724 5955. Decent
basic accommodation if a
shade on the noisy side.

WHERE TO EAT

Ajloun
A handful of establishments
selling basic meals can be
found in the town centre.
Bonita Restaurant, located on
the hill heading up towards
the castle, tel: 02 642 0981.
There is an excellent view of
the castle from the terrace,
and a decent selection of
Arab food including chicken
and meat, mezes and salads.
The kebabs are first class.

Jerash
Jerash Rest House, beside the
visitor centre at the ruins, tel:
02 635 1437. The rest house
is air conditioned and the
food is good, but they charge
a premium because of their
convenient location.
Lebanese House, lies about
750m (820yd) from the
hippodrome and is reached
by taking the Ajloun Road
and then the first south
turning off it – there are no
signposts; tel: 02 635 1301,

www.lebanese-house.com
A lot of Jordanians eat here.

TOURS AND EXCURSIONS

Jordan Circle Tours, Jebel
Amman, Al-Hayyek Street
(opposite Housing Bank),
Amman, tel: 06 464 3017,
www.jct.com.jo
Abercrombie & Kent Jordan,
Abdullah Bin Abbas Street
(opposite Orchid's Hotel),
Amman, tel: 06 566 5465,
www.akdmc.com
Al-Thuraya Travel & Tours,
PO Box 1883, Amman
11821, tel: 06 553 5525,
www.althurayatravel.net
Jordan Tracks, PO Box 468,
Aqaba, tel: 7964 82801,
www.jordantracks.com
Saleem Ali and his family
operate the only Bedouin-
owned tourist agency in
Jordan, based in Wadi Rum.
They also organize tours and
excursions throughout Jordan.

USEFUL CONTACTS

Emergency calls, tel: 196.
British Embassy,
tel: 06 590 9200.
US Embassy,
tel: 06 590 6000.
Al-Khalidi Medical Centre,
tel: 06 464 4281.

AS SALT	J	F	M	A	M	J	J	A	S	O	N	D
AVERAGE TEMP. °F	54	54	64	68	77	82	84	86	82	79	68	55
AVERAGE TEMP. °C	12	12	17	20	25	28	29	30	28	26	20	13
RAINFALL in	6	6	3.6	0.8	0.1	0	0	0	0	1.6	2.4	6
RAINFALL mm	150	150	90	20	2.5	0	0	0	0	40	60	150
DAYS OF RAINFALL	10	10	6	2	1	0	0	0	0	1	4	10

قصر الأزرق

بناه الرومان و عام بناه العرب (عز الدين ايبك)
خلال دور الصيين و سكنه لورانس

QASR AL AZRAQ
BUILT BY THE ROMANS REBUILT BY
ARABS UNDER IZZ ED DIN AYBAK
DURING THE CRUSADES .
AND USED BY LAWRENCE .

4
East of Amman & the Desert Castles

East of Amman is a sparsely populated desert plain bordered by Iraq, Syria and **Saudi Arabia**. Its varied landscape changes from **limestone**-strewn desert to **black basalt** and then **sand**. It was once rich in **wildlife**, including **gazelle**, **ostrich** and the white **Arabian oryx**, but overgrazing, hunting and the pumping of water destroyed their habitat and now they survive only on nature reserves.

The **Romans** were first to build here – a series of forts along the border of their Arabian province. Then in the 7th and 8th centuries the **Umayyads** constructed the scattered, diverse buildings that now illustrate the beginnings of secular **Islamic art and architecture**.

We call them **Desert Castles** but originally they would have been caravan stations, trading posts and meeting places. Once linked by caravan trails, many of them now stand on or near main highways making it possible to visit several on a circular day trip from Amman. This can be done as part of an organized trip arranged through a travel agent, by hiring a taxi and driver for the day or, for the adventurous, renting a car and driving yourself.

Leave Amman through its southern industrial suburb of **Sahab** and continue along **Southern Highway 40** toward **Al-Azraq al-Janubi**. From there **Highway 5** heads north to **As Safawi** before turning left onto **Highway 10** and heading west towards **Mafraq**. Some castles lie deep in the desert and can only be reached using a four-wheel-drive vehicle with an experienced guide, a compass and sufficient food and water.

DON'T MISS

*** Qasr al-Kharrana: magnificent, intact and it looks like a fort.
*** Qasr Amra: this former bath house with its exquisite frescoes is a World Heritage site.
*** Qasr al-Azraq: Lawrence of Arabia's headquarters during the Great Arab Revolt.
*** Umm al-Jimal: visiting this largely deserted black basalt city near the Syrian border is a true 'Indiana Jones' type of adventure.

Opposite: *Qasr al-Azraq, the headquarters of Lawrence of Arabia during the Arab Revolt.*

QASR AL-MUWAQQAR

This is the first castle to be encountered on leaving Amman but it has little to offer. It was built, as a caravan station, during the reign of **Caliph Yazid II** (719–723CE) on a strategic hilltop near the junction of several desert tracks. All that remain are a few low walls between some village houses. Some capitals decorated with acanthus leaves and **Kufic** inscriptions and an ancient water gauge recovered from the site are on display in the Amman Archaeological Museum.

Qasr al-Kharrana ★★★

This is the first complete building encountered on the **Desert Castle Circuit**. The first sign that you are approaching it is a series of radio pylons on the left-hand side of the road. But there is little chance of missing the turn-off as the outline of the building soon comes into view. And it does look like a castle. It is **square**, has **high walls**, **corner towers** and what looks like **arrow slits**. In reality it was probably an ornate **caravanserai**. Archaeologists and historians are still arguing over it, so you can make up your own mind.

The towers are too small to have been defensive and are more likely an architectural device for buttressing the walls. Similarly, the arrow slits are too narrow to have been effective and were probably included for lighting and ventilation. According to an inscription it was built in 711CE.

If it's not already open, the custodian will open the doors and let you in. Afterwards return to the **Bedouin** tent by the car park, buy some postcards or have a cup of tea or a soft drink. Open daily during daylight hours.

Below: *Qasr al-Kharrana. It looks like a castle – it is square, has high walls, corner towers and arrow slits – but was probably a caravanserai.*

Qasr Amra ★★★

Situated on the left-hand side of Highway 40 from Kharrana, this is one of Jordan's three **World Heritage sites**. It was built at the time of **Caliph Walid I** (705–715CE) as a bath house.

The main building has three barrel-vaulted halls. Inside, all of the walls are covered with exquisite frescoes. Just beyond the entrance door is the audience chamber, and facing you, the Caliph on his throne. The south wall has images of the other rulers of the time, including Roderick the Visigoth, Negus of Abyssinia, the Byzantine Emperor, and

Krisa, ruler of Sassania. Other paintings include scenes of dancing, hunting, bathing, cupids and musicians. One of the fascinating things about this artwork is the fact that living beings are portrayed, something that is prohibited in Islam. This chamber was probably used for feasts and meetings. An antechamber leads to the bath, which has a steam room with a domed ceiling with a fresco map of the heavens. Open daily during daylight hours.

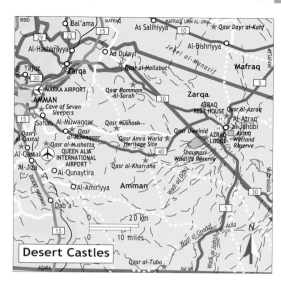

Azraq **

Azraq Oasis lies at the crossroads of several routes across this semi-arid desert. Four springs supply the **oasis** with water and its name. Azraq means blue and once these pools were. Over the last 20 years large-scale pumping of water to Amman has drained the aquifers and now the water is muddy and brackish, the springs have all but dried up, and the palms are dying.

Azraq Wetland Reserve **

This includes several pools, a seasonally flooded marshland and a large mudflat which provides a seasonal habitat for a wide variety of **birds**. A million migrating, breeding and wintering birds come here. Some are just resting on a stopover while others remain throughout the winter to breed in the protected areas. There is a small visitors' centre with an audiovisual production which tells the story of this ancient oasis and the modern threats to its existence. The wetland reserve is managed by the **Royal Society for the Conservation of Nature**. Open daily, 08:00–19:00.

QASR MUSHASH

This, another fairly ruined site lying some distance north of the main highway on an unmarked track, will only be of interest to those with a serious interest in archaeological sites. The remains are scattered over an area in excess of 2km^2 (1 sq mile) and consist of 18 buildings. One may have been a **palace**. It was square in shape, surrounded by walls and its **central courtyard** led to 13 rooms.

Above: *Qasr al-Azraq. This was T E Lawrence's 'blue fort on its rock above the rustling palms' which became his head-quarters during the Great Arab Revolt in 1917–18.*

QASR AL-TUBA

This is the most fascinating of the castles and the most remote – there's a sign pointing to a dirt track on the right just before Qasr al-Kharrana. It's 46km (29 miles) away over very rough country and should not be attempted without a four-wheel-drive vehicle and a guide. This was built by **Caliph Walid II** around 743CE to cater for trading caravans; in essence, it was a motorway service station of its time. It's a large, rectangular walled com-pound containing a number of vaulted rooms.

Shaumari Wildlife Reserve ★★★

Just fifteen minutes' drive along Highway 5 south of Azraq a sign-post indicates a right turn onto a rough track leading to the wildlife reserve famed for its **Operation Oryx**. The oryx is a species of antelope, and the Arabian oryx is the smallest of them. This white oryx once roamed throughout the deserts of Arabia and the Fertile Crescent but was almost hunted out of existence. The last known wild Arabian Oryx was killed by hunters in Oman in 1972. Prior to this the **World Wildlife Fund** had established a survival herd with three animals from Oman, one from London, one from Kuwait and four from Saudi Arabia. It was from this herd that the oryx were reintroduced to Jordan in 1978. There are now 200 of them protected in this reserve. Open daily, 08:00–19:00.

Qasr al-Azraq ★★★

About 13km (8 miles) north of Azraq, on Highway 5 heading towards Iraq, is the fortress of Qasr al-Azraq. It was completed in its present form by the **Mamelukes** in the 13th century from an earlier fort dating from **Roman** times. Built of local black basalt, it stands guard over Azraq's water supplies and trade links. But its main claim to fame is as 'the blue fort on its rock above the rustling palms', which became the desert head-quarters of **Lawrence of Arabia** during the **Great Arab Revolt** in 1917–18.

It's an almost square building with huge walls enclosing a central courtyard. The main entrance is into a vestibule through a massive three-ton hinged basalt door which was installed in Roman times and is still operational. Look at the bottom where the stone hinge enters the floor slab. It is kept well greased by the custodian. There's a similar door on the back wall but it is seized shut.

Above the vestibule is the room that was used by Lawrence when he was here. It was winter then and in the *Seven Pillars of Wisdom* he describes how 'On stormy nights, we brought in brushwood and dung and lit a great fire in the middle of the floor. About it would be drawn carpets and the saddle sheepskins, and in its light we would tell over our own battles, or hear the visitors' traditions.' The fort suffered severe damage during an earthquake in 1927 but is otherwise as Lawrence would have found it. It is open daily during daylight hours.

Qasr Dayr al-Kahf *

Continue north on Highway 5 from Qasr al-Azraq to **As Safawi**, the largest town in Eastern Badia. There's nothing of interest here except the Junction with Highway 10. You need to turn left here but the junction is not obvious. If you miss it there's nothing of note until the border with Iraq.

Continue heading east along Highway 10 until you reach **Al-Bishriyya**, then turn right onto a minor road signposted for Qasr Dayr al-Khaf. It's a very small village and the fort is easy to find. Built by the Romans in the early years of the 4th century BCE it was a link in the chain of forts built along the **Strata Diocletiana** as a defence against Arab raiders. It lies a mere 5km (3 miles) south of the Syrian border.

> **QASR AL-MUSHATTA**
>
> This is similar in style to Qasr al-Tuba but was never fully completed. It's a large brick-walled compound with 23 round towers spaced along the walls. Inside there is a mosque and a square palace with vaulted ceilings and ornate decoration. It's situated south of Amman in the precincts of the airport and reached by taking the perimeter road to the end of the north runway.

Below: *Qasr Dayr al-Kahf was built, in the early years of the 4th century* BCE, *by the Romans as one of their chain of defensive forts along the Strata Diocletiana.*

ROMAN ROAD

During the Roman occupation a road linked the forts and settlements along what is now the Syrian border. These forts and linking road guarded the main trade route between Syria and Mesopotamia. Remains of this road can still be seen near the village of Al-Ba'ij, about fifteen minutes' drive west of Umm al-Jimal.

QASR AL-QASTAL

What remains of this once magnificent palace sits adjacent to a modern village of the same name. It's one of the easiest of the palaces to reach, being a mere 100m (109yd) west of the Desert Highway heading south from Amman. It's also one of the oldest of the Umayyad settlements and includes a mosque, palace, small houses, baths and a cemetery. The cemetery is the oldest Muslim graveyard in Jordan.

Its Arabic name means the 'Monastery of the Caves'. It's a large black building with several of the walls intact and a magnificent barrel-vaulted passageway leading to the interior courtyard. This is so far off the tourist trail that you'll likely have it all to yourself with the possible exception of the herd of goats that graze in and around it.

Umm al-Jimal ★★★

Within spitting distance of the Syrian border sits a strange city built of black basalt. It can be reached by going along the back road from Qasr Dayr al-Kahf or by turning off the As Safawi-Mafraq highway.

It was built about 2000 years ago, probably by the **Nabateans**. They were traders and under them Umm al-Jimal became a major centre for trading caravans, which may explain its name. Translated from Arabic it means 'Mother of Camels'. A large, vacant area in the city centre was where the caravans camped.

When the Romans took over they incorporated it in their defensive line of forts. Ten minutes' driving west on the back road from the ruins will take you to **Al-Ba'ij** and the remains of the Roman road, the **Via Nova Traiana**. Although it is contemporaneous with Jerash, you won't find any grand buildings and monuments here. This is how the ordinary people of that period lived. There may have been a period of instability around the 3rd century CE as the inhabitants erected a

perimeter wall at that time. It was constructed of the familiar black basalt but also incorporated a number of **tombstones**. With the coming of the Byzantines and Christianity, several **churches** were erected. But mainly it was a prosperous trading and agricultural city. There are several **reservoirs** on the site – some open, others covered. These collected and stored the rainwater that provided the inhabitants with all of their needs and also provided irrigation for the surrounding fields.

Various events took their toll on Umm al-Jimal, including plague and further invasions, but it was the **earthquake** of 747 CE that finally ended 700 years of occupation.

Excavation and restoration is an ongoing process but there's a lot to see, including sections of the old stables, the arched wall of the **West Church**, a 5th-century **Barracks** with a massive stone door similar to that at Azraq, and a **Byzantine tower**.

Above: *Qasr Hammam al-Sarah contains the remains of a bathing complex.*
Opposite: *Umm al-Jimal, an ancient Nabatean trading city.*

Qasr al-Hallabat ★

This was originally built as hilltop fort by the Romans during the 2nd and 3rd centuries CE. By the 7th century it had become a monastery, then a makeover from the Umayyads added white limestone to the black basalt and decorated the interior with frescoes and carvings. They also added a mosque, mosaic floors and an extensive irrigation system. From the previous site you can get here by turning left off the main highway and heading south towards **Ad Dulayl**.

Just past the fort, heading east, the remains of the bathing complex of **Qasr Hammam al-Sarah** are worth visiting, even though the marble and mosaics that once decorated them are no more. Continuing along this road brings you to a junction with Highway 30 and a right turn will take you to **Zarqa** and the motorway south to Amman.

QASR UWEINID

This was a Roman outpost constructed from black basalt to protect Wadi Sirhan, a valuable trade and communication route. This route runs southeast from Azraq to cross into what is now Saudi Arabia to the wells of Maybuu. According to an inscribed lintel found at the site the outpost was built early in the 3rd century CE. In later times it became a caravanserai on the trade route from Arabia to Amman. It lies south of Azraq but a four-wheel-drive vehicle is needed to visit it.

East of Amman and the Desert Castles at a Glance

Spring (March–May) and autumn (September–October) are the best times to visit. In summer the days can get very hot and the nights chilly, while winter is generally cold. What little rain falls in the Eastern Desert tends to do so in the winter months.

Because of a lack of quality hotels most people touring this area do so from a base in Amman. The distances are not great and it is possible to do the circular trip of the Desert Castles in a single day, although two would be preferable. There is some budget accommodation and there are government rest houses for those who want to spend more time in the area.

There is public transport in the Eastern Desert but it requires considerable planning and not all of the Desert Castles are accessible. **Buses** from Amman go to Zarqa and from there buses run east to Azraq. To visit Umm al-Jimal you will need to take the bus from Amman to Mafraq and then change for one heading east to As Safawi. There is the option of joining an **organized tour** or renting a **taxi** in Amman or Madaba for the day. This is best done through your hotel as the staff will be able to arrange a reliable

driver. By far the best and most exciting way to tour this area is to **hire a car** from a local company like **Rent a Reliable Car** and drive yourself. You'll find them at: 19 Fawzi Al-Qaweqji Street, PO Box 960643, Amman 11196, tel: 06 592 9676. The contact is Mohammed Hallak.

Minibuses have no set timetables; buses usually depart when full. Journey times are approximate: Zarqa to Azraq 1 hour 20 minutes, Amman to Mafraq 1 hour, Mafraq to Umm al-Jimal 30 minutes, Mafraq to Zarqa 30 minutes.

Amman
LUXURY
Crowne Plaza Hotel, King Faysal Bin Abdul Azia Street, Amman, 950555, tel: 06 551 0001, www.cpamman.com Thirty minutes' drive from Queen Alia International Airport and situated right in the heart of the city centre.
Holiday Inn, Madina Al-Munawarah Street, PO Box 941825, Amman, 11194, tel: 06 552 8822, www.holidayinn.com Located in western Amman, close to the main shopping centres and just 30 minutes' drive from the airport.
Kempinski, Abdul Hameed Shouman Street, Shmeisani, PO Box 941045, Amman, 11194, tel: 06 520 0200, www.kempinski-amman.com Unashamed luxury with fine

dining and splendid views. One of the best hotels in the city centre.
Le Meridien, Queen Noor Street, Shmeisani, PO Box 950629, Amman, 11195, tel: 06 569 6511, www.starwood hotels.com/lemeridien/property/overview/index.html?propertyID=1878 Another world-class hotel in the heart of the city, with a choice of international cuisine including food from Lebanon, Japan and Mongolia.
Marriott, Shmeissani Issam Ajluni Street, PO Box 926333, Amman, 11190, tel: 06 560 7607, www.marriott.co.uk/hotels/travel/ammjr-amman-marriott-hotel/ Centrally located in the Shmeisani area, this is ideal for both business and leisure travellers, being close to tourist attractions, shopping and the business district.
Sheraton Amman Al-Nabil Hotel & Towers, 5th Circle, PO Box 840064, Amman, 11184, tel: 06 593 4111, www.starwoodhotels.com/sheraton/property/overview/index.html?propertyID=1239 This magnificent white stone building is located on a hilltop site in the heart of Amman's embassy and business district.

Azraq
MID-RANGE
Al-Sayad Hotel, half a kilometre south of Qasr al-Azraq,

tel: 05 264 7611. This can only be described as an experience. Neat gardens, mock Islamic architecture and a rather bizarre decor combine to give this establishment a surreal atmosphere. Having said that it is clean, has a decent restaurant and is reasonably priced.

BUDGET

Azraq Lodge, tel: 05 383 5017. This RSCN guesthouse is situated 1km (0.6 mile) from the Azraq Wetland Reserve. Bookings can be made either via the RSCN headquarters in Amman or at the lodge itself.
Azraq Rest House, tel: 05 383 4006. Signposted from Azraq, off the main highway and down a 1500m (1640yd) tree-lined avenue. The rest house is a government-run establishment.
Al-Zoubi Hotel, tel: 05 383 5012. Look for this behind the Refa'I Restaurant in al-Azraq al-Janubi. Clean and basic, but has *en-suite* rooms and a decent price.
Al-Zoubi Hotel, head south of Al-Azraq al-Janubi for about 22km (14 miles) to reach the Jafr interchange where the roads from southern Jordan and Saudi Arabia meet. The hotel is remote (it doesn't even have a phone), and although it is located in the middle of a desert, it has its own well-watered green garden. The rooms are clean.

WHERE TO EAT

There is a scarcity of decent eateries in this area, so carry plenty of water and enough food for your journey. Azraq lies about halfway round the Desert Castle circuit and has basic cafés or restaurants on the main street. Most serve just chicken, beef, hummus and bread. Cheap, tasty and filling falafel can also be bought from roadside stalls.
Azraq Rest House provides basic simple fare, but just a bit to the north of their turnoff is the excellent **Azraq Palace Tourist Restaurant**. This is the best place to stop for a meal. The lunch buffet is great value and will give you the chance to try traditional Arab *mansaf*.

TOURS AND EXCURSIONS

Jordan Circle Tours, Jebel Amman, Al-Hayyek Street (opposite Housing Bank), Amman, tel: 06 464 3017, www.jct.com.jo
Abercrombie & Kent Jordan, Abdullah Bin Abbas Street (opposite Orchid's Hotel), Amman, tel: 06 566 5465, www.akdmc.com
Al-Thuraya Travel & Tours, PO Box 1883, Amman

11821, tel: 06 553 5525, www.althurayatravel.net
Jordan Tracks, PO Box 468, Aqaba, tel: 7964 82801, www.jordantracks.com
Saleem Ali and his family operate the only Bedouin-owned tourist agency in Jordan, based in Wadi Rum. They also organize tours and excursions throughout Jordan.

USEFUL CONTACTS

Emergency calls, tel: 196.
British Embassy, tel: 06 590 9200.
US Embassy, tel: 06 590 6000.
Al-Khalidi Medical Centre, tel: 06 464 4281.
Tourism Development Board Office, Queen Alia International Airport, Amman, tel: 06 445 2063.
Jordan Tourist Board, Amman, tel: 06 567 8294.
Royal Society for the Conservation of Nature (RSCN), tel: 06 533 7931.
Sale Tax Return Office, Queen Alia International Airport, tel: 06 445 1552.
Royal Jordanian Airlines, reservations, tel: 06 510 0000; flight information: www.amman-airport.com

AS SAFAWI	J	F	M	A	M	J	J	A	S	O	N	D
AVERAGE TEMP. °F	57	59	66	77	86	93	100	100	93	84	70	59
AVERAGE TEMP. °C	14	15	19	25	30	34	38	38	34	29	21	15
RAINFALL in	4.8	4.8	4.8	1	0.4	0	0	0	0	1.6	0.4	0.6
RAINFALL mm	12	12	12	2.5	1	0	0	0	0	4	1	1.5
DAYS OF RAINFALL	1	1	1	1	1	0	0	0	0	1	1	1

5
Madaba & the Dead Sea

The land of the Dead Sea plain and its surrounding hills has witnessed some of the greatest events in **biblical history**. The Patriarch Abraham arrived here from Mesopotamia, Esau sold his birthright to Jacob for a bowl of soup, and God rained fire and brimstone on the cities of Sodom and Gomorrah. Moses died and was buried here after seeing the promised land he had been told he would never enter. It is where Joshua led the Children of Israel across the River Jordan into Canaan, where the prophet Elijah ascended into heaven in his chariot of fire and his successor, Elisha, cured lepers by the river. John the Baptist lived and preached here and it is where he baptized Jesus before being beheaded by King Herod Antipas. Much later the Prophet Mohammed travelled here on his night-time journey from Mecca to Jerusalem.

This was the biblical kingdom of the **Moabites** where great battles were fought. Over three thousand years ago **Madaba** was a Moabite border city. One of its many churches contains the oldest known map of the Middle East. The lowest point on planet earth is here by the **Dead Sea**. This landlocked water mass is so salty it is incapable of sustaining life but is a valuable source of minerals, health and beauty products. At its northern end the Dead Sea is a rapidly expanding tourist area with hotels, beaches and a conference centre. In stark contrast, the southern end contains the vast evaporation ponds of the **Arab Potash Company**, one of the world's leading exporters of potash.

DON'T MISS

*** Madaba Mosaic Map: the oldest known map of the Middle East.
*** Madaba Archaeological Park: exquisite Byzantine mosaics and the remains of a Roman road.
*** Mount Nebo: where Moses saw the promised land and where he is buried.
*** Bethany Beyond the Jordan: where John the Baptist immersed Jesus in the water of the Jordan.
*** The Dead Sea: where it is impossible to sink.
*** John the Baptist Church: where Jesus left his clothes.

Opposite: *Mount Nebo, Moses Memorial Church.*

MADABA ***

This small town, 30km (19 miles) southwest of Amman, is a good alternative base for exploring the Dead Sea region. Part of the King's Highway, it is a major attraction in its own right. A **Christian community** was in existence here as far back as 451CE when the Acts of the Council of Chalcedon mention Gaiano 'Bishop of the Medabeni'.

The **Persian invasion** of 614CE badly affected the economy of towns like Madaba, but it was the earthquake in 747 that destroyed its buildings. The population of the town moved away and Madaba lay abandoned until the late 19th century.

In 1880 Muslim tribes expelled several Arab Christian families from Al-Karak. Led by two Italian priests, they moved north to occupy the ruins of Madaba. But the Ottoman authorities would only grant them permission to build their houses on the sites of former Christian churches.

It was while clearing ground for these new houses that the fabulous **Byzantine mosaics** of Madaba were uncovered. The priests, recognizing their importance, made sure that they were preserved. Archaeological research uncovered other mosaics in the area and their study has resulted in Madaba becoming known as Jordan's 'City of Mosaics'.

Today Christians make up a large part of Madaba's population, which explains why you will see so many women walking the streets without the traditional Islamic headscarf.

WEAVING IN MADABA

Madaba is an important centre for the hand-loom weaving of kilims. The quality varies considerably, from coarse rugs made of thick wool to the more expensive articles painstakingly constructed from fine threads. Wander along any of the back streets of the town and keep a look out for signs advertising weaving and rugs. That's where you'll find the weavers working in the time-honoured fashion on their traditional hand looms, either in their shop or in a back room.

The Madaba Map ★★★

This famous mosaic map of the Middle East can be found within the **Church of St George**. It was discovered in 1896 and when the archaeologists who excavated it published their findings the following year Madaba became the focus of international attention. The map was created around the 6th century CE and would originally have been approximately 25m by 5m (82ft x 16ft) in size and would have contained over two million separate stones. The fragment that has survived clearly shows Jerusalem and the Church of the Holy Sepulchre, the Dead Sea, the Jordan River, Nablus, Hebron, Jericho, Egypt and the Nile, Turkey and Lebanon. Open Monday–Thursday and Saturday, 08:30–18:00, Friday and Sunday 10:30–18:00. There is an admission charge.

Archaeological Park ★★★

The Archaeological Park is in the centre of Madaba and runs along part of the Roman road that once crossed the city. This complex includes the **Church of the Virgin**, a small museum and a Byzantine mansion.

Inside is perhaps the finest collection of mosaics in Jordan, including a Hellenistic mosaic recovered from Herod's Palace. The floor mosaic of the Church of the Virgin is from the Abbasid period in the 8th century CE. Its distinctive decorations surround a central medallion with an inscription. Round the edges of this are the remains of the images of flowers that were part

> **THE EXODUS**
>
> The Book of Exodus in the Bible describes how Moses and Aaron led the Hebrew slaves out of Egypt to return to Israel. The Jewish Feast of the Passover is from that time. The Hebrews had followed Joseph to Egypt when he was vizier but after his death the Egyptians enslaved them for four centuries. Moses, with the assistance of a series of plagues sent by God, negotiated their release.

Opposite: *A section of the 6th-century Madaba Map of the Holy Land with Jerusalem at its centre.*

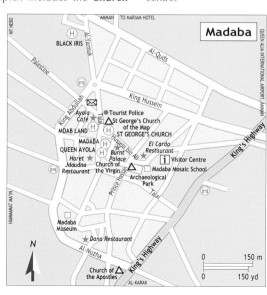

MOSES

When the Egyptian Pharaoh ordered the death of all newborn Hebrew boys, Moses's mother placed him in a basket and floated it in the River Nile. The basket was recovered by the Pharaoh's daughter and she adopted the baby. As an adult, Moses killed an Egyptian who was beating Hebrew slaves, and was obliged to flee. He spent many years tending sheep until, according to biblical accounts, he was commanded by God to lead the Israelites out of Egypt.

of the original floor when the church was built in the 6th century.

The **Hippolytus Hall** formed part of a rich Byzantine mansion which was demolished when the Church of the Virgin was built. The mosaic floor of this hall is regarded as one of the great masterpieces of the Madaba mosaicists. Its central theme illustrates the myth of Phaedra and Hippolytus, although only the image of Phaedra has survived.

The park is a short walk from the Church of St George and the admission ticket also covers entrance to the **Madaba Museum** and the **Church of the Apostles**. Open daily, 08:00–18:30 (16:00 in winter).

Mosaic School ★★

This was formed from abandoned buildings within what is now the Archaeological Park. It is where the technicians and conservators who repair and restore Jordan's mosaics are trained. The first 13 students graduated from here in 1995. The course lasts for two years. Students start by learning how to make mosaics, then move on to copying details from some of the better known ones. Examples of their work can be seen around the school complex. Then they proceed to the work of conservation and restoration. During the summer the senior students work on archaeological sites throughout Jordan.

Below: *This and other examples of the work completed by students of the Madaba Mosaic School are on display throughout the complex.*

Church of the Apostles ★★

At the southern entrance to Madaba, near the King's Highway, are the remains of the **Church of the Apostles**. This Byzantine church was built around 578CE and contains the mosaic called the *Personification of the Sea*. In it a female form surrounded by mythical creatures emerges from the ocean. Open daily 08:00–18:30.

Madaba Museum ★★★

This is a courtyard development down a small alley not far from the Archaeological Park. The museum was created from several houses and during renovation work many mosaics were uncovered. Also on display are collections of pottery, coins and costume from throughout Jordan's history. The museum also has one of several copies of the **Mesha Stele** (*see* panel, page 13) that are located throughout Jordan. Open Wednesday–Monday 09:00–17:00 (10:00–16:00 on holidays).

Above: *The Moses Memorial Church, built over the original basilica by the Franciscans, has a series of stained-glass windows.*

MOUNT NEBO ★★★

This is one of the most important Christian and Jewish sites in Jordan. According to the Bible 'Moses went up from the plains of Moab to Mount Nebo, the top of Pisgah which is opposite Jericho.' From there he was able to gaze upon the **promised land** that God had told him he would not be allowed to enter.

Today there is a large viewing area where visitors can look across the Dead Sea, the Desert of Judah and the mountains of Judea and Samaria. On the far side of the Dead Sea, **Qumran** – where the Dead Sea Scrolls were discovered – is easily picked out, and further north the city of **Jericho**. On clear days it is even possible to see Bethlehem from here, as well as the Mount of Olives and Dome of the Rock in Jerusalem.

The nearby **Brazen Serpent Monument** was created by Italian artist Giovanni Fantoni and was inspired by the bronze serpent Moses created in the wilderness and also by Christ's cross.

THE TEN COMMANDMENTS

These 'rules', according to biblical tradition, were written by God on two stone tablets and given to Moses on Mount Sinai during the Exodus. However, when Moses returned to his people he found that they had made a golden calf and were worshipping it. In anger he smashed the tablets. Later he obtained two more tablets which were placed in a sacred container called the Ark of the Covenant.

حراسة الاراضى المقدسة
الآثار الأثرية
جبل نيبو- صياغة
مقام النبي موسى
وقف مسيحى

FRANCISCAN CUSTODY OF THE HOLY LAND
MOUNT NEBO SIYAGHA
MEMORIAL OF MOSES
CHRISTIAN HOLY PLACE

Above: *This inscribed stone was erected by the Franciscans at the Monastery of Siyagha where Moses died.*

Mount Nebo has several peaks. Two of them, **Siyagha** and **al-Mukhayyat**, were purchased by the Franciscans in 1932 and a year later they unearthed the remains of a church dating back to the 4th century CE. Several years were spent excavating the site and building the **Moses Memorial Church**. Inside are mosaics uncovered during the excavations, including a floor which was laid in 531CE. This was discovered by chance in 1976 when a later mosaic which had been laid on top of it was removed for restoration work.

Near the chapel is an olive tree planted as a peace symbol by Pope John Paul II who visited during his pilgrimage in 2000.

According to Jewish and Christian tradition Moses died here and, as he was buried by God, the site of his grave is unknown. Open daily 07:00–19:00 (17:00 in winter).

BETHANY BEYOND THE JORDAN **

Few places on earth are as atmospheric as this spot on the Jordan River where John baptized Jesus Christ. According to the Bible, **John the Baptist** lived, preached and carried out baptisms in the village of Bethany on 'the other side of the Jordan'. It was a different Bethany from the village of the same name, near Jerusalem, where Lazarus was raised from the dead.

Across the river you can see the city of Jericho. According to biblical accounts it was here, at a ford in the Jordan called Beit 'Abara or Bethabara, that God stopped the river from flowing so that **Joshua** could lead his people across the river into Canaan. This is one of Christianity's most sacred places for as well as Joshua, **Elijah**, **Elisha**, **John the Baptist** and **Jesus Christ** all used this crossing point, and from the early years of the Christian era this was an important pilgrims' route.

Archaeologists knew that Bethany was somewhere in this area but for years it was a closed military zone. Following the peace treaty between Jordan and Israel in 1994, they were able to undertake a detailed study. They analysed the accounts of medieval travellers, studied descriptions in the Bible, then started exploratory digging. Eventually at **Wadi al-Kharrar**, the head of a lush valley east of the Jordan, they uncovered what the Arabs call **al-Maghtas**, the **Place of Dipping**.

Come here in the early morning, before the crowds arrive and before the sun gets too high. It is easy to look across the landscape and imagine the wild figure of John the Baptist, waiting by his pool as the robed and bearded Jesus walks slowly towards him. Open daily, 08:00–16:00 (until 18:00 in summer). Last entry one hour before closing.

The Baptist's Spring ★★

This spring was described in antiquity as flowing from Tell Mar Elias and running to an area near the Baptist's church. The water from the spring was used by pilgrims

JOSHUA

Joshua succeeded Moses and led the Children of Israel across the River Jordan and into the Promised Land of Canaan. There he commanded a particularly bloody conquest of the land. Starting with the city of Jericho, he had his troops march round it for seven days and then the walls collapsed. The Israelites then slaughtered all of the men, women, children and even the livestock. After the conquest of Canaan, Joshua divided the land amongst the tribes of Israel.

Below: *The Baptism site at Bethany Beyond the Jordan where John baptized Jesus and acknowledged him as the Messiah.*

for drinking and for baptism. In the height of the summer it is often dry. There were several pools filled by
the water from the spring. A large stone-built pool was
uncovered during the excavations and was probably
used for baptisms during the **Byzantine** period.

John's Cave **

A 'laura' was a monastery of individual monks cells.
From the 7th century we have one writer's account of
the tale of a monk travelling on pilgrimage to Sinai
from Jerusalem. After crossing the Jordan, he contracted
a fever and sheltered in a cave at Bethany Beyond the
Jordan. John the Baptist appeared to him in a dream
and told him, 'This little cave is greater than Mount
Sinai. Our Lord Jesus Christ himself has come in here
to pay me a visit.' When the monk recovered from his
illness he abandoned his pilgrimage and converted the
cave into a church.

John the Baptist Church ***

This church and monastery were built at the time of the
Emperor Anastasius (491–518CE) and archaeologists

Right: *There are many
caves located around the
Baptism site at Bethany
Beyond the Jordan.
St John may have used
one or all of them.*

believe they are the ruins of **Bethabara**, built on the site where the baptism of Jesus was believed to have taken place and also the exact spot where he left his clothes.

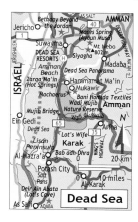

Elijah's Hill ★

At the start of Wadi al-Kharrar, near the monastic compound known as the 'laura', is a hill referred to in the Bible as **Hermon**. Many early writers refer to it, including one Theodosius who described it in 530CE as follows: 'Where my Lord was baptized there is, on the far side of the Jordan, the "little hill" called Hermon, where Saint Elijah was taken up.' In Arabic it is **Jebel Mar Elias**, the hill of Elijah where, according to tradition, the prophet ascended into heaven in a chariot of fire.

Church of John Paul II ★★★

Named to commemorate Pope John Paul II's visit here on 21 March 2000, this church was actually built much earlier – some time between the 5th and 6th centuries CE. It had a mosaic floor with cross decorations, and arches which supported the roof. One of them has been recreated. Originally it was used for prayer and worship by incoming pilgrims.

THE DEAD SEA ★★★

Sitting 400m (1312ft) below sea level, the Dead Sea is the **lowest point on earth**. No visitor to Jordan should leave without having a dip in it. It's as near as it is possible to get to walking on water. The sea is so dense that it is impossible to sink. Even swimming is difficult because the body is lifted too high out of the water.

The Dead Sea is 75km (47 miles) in length and 16km (10 miles) across at its widest point. It is fed by the Jordan River but has no outlet and that, coupled with the high temperatures, results in rapid evaporation which accounts for its high salt and mineral content. Dead Sea water contains about 350 grams of salt per kilogram compared to the 40 grams per kilogram present in the water of the world's oceans.

THE LISAN PENINSULA

This is a massive salt layer jutting out into the Dead Sea from its the southern shores. On both the Jordanian and Israeli sides of the sea, huge salt evaporation pans have been created to extract minerals from the water. These include potash, sodium chloride, bromine and caustic soda. The Israelis have a power plant which also enables them to produce magnesium.

Above: *The Dead Sea has such a high salt content that it is impossible to sink in it but it makes even small cuts and grazes sting like mad.*

DEAD SEA PRODUCTS

The water in the Dead Sea is rich in calcium, magnesium, potassium and bromine. Bath salts from the Dead Sea are used to treat skin diseases like psoriasis, while the application of Dead Sea mud is supposed to relieve the pain from joint inflammation and ease stiffness. Dead Sea cosmetic products are also believed to help restore skin vitality and tighten the pores to produce a smoother surface and reduce the effects of wrinkles.

Since the time of Herod the Great the **natural elements** of the Dead Sea have been used in treating various skin disorders. But a word of warning: if you have any small cuts or grazes on your skin, you'll become painfully aware of them the minute you hit the water. The high salt content will make them sting like mad. You will even be made aware of small cuts you did not know you had.

Unfortunately, the increased use by Jordan and Israel of water from the River Jordan has considerably reduced the flow into the Dead Sea. Water is evaporating faster than it is being replenished, and since 1930 the level of the Dead Sea has dropped by 17m (56ft) and its overall area has shrunk by one third. There is, however, talk of Israel and Jordan building a canal from the Red Sea to halt and reverse this decline.

In biblical times the plain along the southeast coast of the Dead Sea was known as the **Valley of Salt**. This is where Abraham and his nephew Lot separated and divided their herds after their journey from Egypt. It was also here that King David 'slew 18,000 Edomites'.

Amman Beach ★★

Lying south of the hotel zone at the northeast end, Amman Beach is the only **public beach** on the Dead Sea. Public buses run here from Amman and drop visitors off in the beach car park. It has a variety of facilities including changing rooms, a restaurant, children's play park and the essential freshwater showers. Open 24/7. There is an admission charge.

Wadi Mujib Nature Reserve **

Stretching from the shores of the Dead Sea to the King's Highway and from Wadi Mujib north to Hammamat Ma'in, this reserve contains seven wadis and a surprising variety of wildlife. The **Nubian ibex** has recently been reintroduced to the wild here, and other animals, including the **Egyptian mongoose** and **Syrian wolf**, are present.

Some of the most spectacular and most demanding trails in Jordan are in this reserve. The **Mujib Trail** is an eight-hour hike along a dry river bed, while the **Malaqi Trail** is a water trail that involves hiking and swimming, not to mention a high level of fitness.

The main visitors' centre is near the Mujib bridge on the Dead Sea Highway south of the hotel zone. All of the trails require pre-booking with the **Royal Society for the Conservation of Nature**, as visitor numbers are strictly controlled.

Bab adh-Dhra *

Not much remains of this once flourishing city other than the outline of its walls and the foundations of a few houses. Back in 2600BCE this was a flourishing settlement, but the discovery of a massive **cemetery** from the early **Bronze Age** marks it as a very important centre. There is enough space in the 20,000 shaft tombs discovered to bury 500,000 people. This site and

GOMORRAH

Some 13km (8 miles) south of Bab adh-Dhra beside the Wadi Numeira is an archaeological site that archaeologists believe may be all that remains of the city of Gomorrah. Excavations have shown that this was burned near the end of the early Bronze Age. Excavations have revealed that the settlement was abandoned but before leaving the residents had prepared it for their eventual return. When it was burned, one of the towers collapsed and the remains of three bodies were found trapped underneath.

THE CITIES OF THE PLAIN

At the time of their destruction, **Sodom** and **Gomorrah** were two of the five cities of the Vale of Siddom by the Dead Sea. The others were Admah, Eboiim and Zoar. Archaeologists have uncovered five sites from the early Bronze Age, all located by small wadis. The site near Safi has been identified by the Madaba Map as being the city of Zoar where Lot and his daughters briefly escaped to before moving to their cave sanctuary.

Left: *Salt deposits build up on the rocks and boulders round the shoreline of the Dead Sea.*

LOT'S WIFE

According to the Bible, when God decided to destroy Sodom and Gomorrah angels told Lot and his family to 'Escape for thy life! Look not behind thee, neither stay thou in all the plain. Escape to the mountain, lest thou be consumed!' Unfortunately, his wife turned round and was allegedly turned into a pillar of salt. Tour buses now stop by the Dead Sea Highway near a pillar of salt known locally as Lot's Wife.

another city nearby were destroyed at the end of the Bronze Age and archaeologists have discovered layers of ash indicating **destruction by fire**. The Dead Sea sits on a major fault line and one hypothesis suggests that an earthquake forced bitumen, petroleum and sulphur into the atmosphere, destroying both settlements. Because of this, some scholars believe that Bab adh-Dhra was the biblical **Sodom**.

'Then the Lord rained upon Sodom and upon Gomorrah brimstone and fire from the Lord out of heaven; And he overthrew those cities, and all the plain, and all the inhabitants of the cities, and that which grew upon the ground.' Genesis 19:24, 25.

Right: *According to popular tradition this pillar of salt by the shores of the Dead Sea was once the lawfully wedded wife of Lot.*

The Bab adh-Dhra site can be reached from the Dead Sea Highway just south of the village of Al-Mazra'a. Turn left onto the road heading to Al-Karak and look for the site on the left about a kilometre from the junction.

Above: *Lot's Cave is a small cave in the mountains above the Dead Sea where he sheltered from the destruction of Sodom and Gommorah.*

Deir Ain Abata (Lot's Cave) **

This hillside cave lies just off the Dead Sea Highway, 2km (1¼ miles) north of the village of As Safi. Tradition maintains that this is where Lot fled with his two daughters after the destruction of Sodom and Gomorrah.

'And Lot went up out of Zoar, and dwelt in the mountain, and his two daughters with him: for he feared to dwell in Zoar: and he dwelt in a cave, he and his two daughters.'

Early Christians built a **monastery** to commemorate the sanctuary, but this was abandoned in the 8th century CE, possibly after it was destroyed in an earthquake. The site overlooks the Dead Sea and houses remnants of a Byzantine monastery. It was rediscovered in the late 20th century and excavations have uncovered artefacts from the **Bronze Age** through to the early **Islamic period**. The climb up the 294 steps from the car park to the cave is a bit on the steep side, but well worth the effort.

Lot's Museum **

This state-of-the-art new museum is located near the entrance to Lot's Cave. Various opening dates have been advanced since 2007, the latest being the summer of 2011. The two-storey shell-shaped building was designed by a local architect and contains an exhibition hall and café. It will cover four main themes: **The Story of Lot**, **The Story of Sugar**, **The Lowest Place on Earth** and **The Peopling of the Ghor**.

LOT'S DAUGHTERS

After they had escaped the devastation of Sodom and Gomorrah, Lot and his daughters sought shelter in a mountain cave by the Dead Sea. His daughters, believing themselves to be the last surviving females, hatched a plan to enable their race to continue. On two nights they got their father drunk and seduced him, each becoming pregnant. They bore Lot two sons, Moab and Ammon, patriarchs of the Moabites and Ammonites.

Madaba and the Dead Sea at a Glance

Spring (March–May) and autumn (September–October) are the best times to visit Madaba and the surrounding Highlands. The days are temperate at around 19–30°C (66–86°F) and most of the rain has fallen in the winter months. The Dead Sea, athough very close, is considerably lower and even in winter temperatures seldom drop below 21°C (70°F). The coolest months are December to March when temperatures are 21–25°C (70–77°F).

Madaba is a mere 30km (19 miles) southwest of Amman and easily reached by bus or taxi. The bus station is a short walk from the town centre. Minibuses run from Muhajireen station to Amman Beach at the Dead Sea from 07:00 to 09:00 each day. The service is only guaranteed on a Friday. At other times the bus will only leave if it has enough passengers.

Buses run from Madaba to Mount Nebo and on to the Dead Sea at al-Shunah al-Janubiyya. From there a connecting bus runs to Amman Beach, the conference centre and the luxury resort hotels. It is also possible to arrange a taxi tour from Madaba taking in Mount Nebo, the Dead Sea and the

Baptism Site. This is best organized through your hotel. Public transport south of the Dead Sea resorts is almost non-existent so renting a self-drive car or hiring a taxi for a day are the best options for exploring this fascinating part of Jordan.

Amman
LUXURY
Kempinski, Abdul Hameed Shouman Street, Shmeisani, PO Box 941045, Amman, 11194, tel: 06 520 0200, www.kempinski-amman.com Unashamed luxury with fine dining and splendid views. One of the best hotels in the city centre.
Le Meridien, Queen Noor Street, Shmeisani, PO Box 950629, Amman, 11195, tel: 06 569 6511, www.starwood hotels.com/lemeridien/ property/overview/index. html?propertyID=1878 Another world-class hotel in the heart of the city, with a choice of international cuisine including food from Lebanon, Japan and Mongolia.
Crowne Plaza Hotel, King Faysal Bin Abdul Azia Street, Amman, 950555, tel: 06 551 0001, www.cpamman.com Thirty minutes' drive from Queen Alia International Airport and situated right in the heart of the city centre.
Holiday Inn, Madina Al-Munawarah Street, PO Box 941825, Amman, 11194,

tel: 06 552 8822, www. holidayinn.com Located in western Amman, close to the main shopping centres and just 30 minutes' drive from the airport.
Sheraton Amman Al-Nabil Hotel & Towers, 5th Circle, PO Box 840064, Amman, 11184, tel: 06 593 4111, www.starwoodhotels.com/ sheraton/property/overview/ index.html?propertyID=1239 This magnificent white stone building is on a hilltop site in the heart of Amman's embassy and business district.

Dead Sea
LUXURY
Kempinski Hotel Ishtar Dead Sea, Dead Sea Road, PO Box 815554, Amman 11180, tel: 05 356 8888, www.kempinski.com/en/ deadsea Without a doubt this is *the* most luxurious hotel in Jordan. It was designed in tribute to the Hanging Gardens of Babylon and draws heavily on Sumerian architecture.
Mövenpick Resort & Spa Dead Sea, Suwayma, Dead Sea Road, PO Box 815538, Amman 11180, tel: 05 356 1111, www.movenpick-deadsea.com Superb modern luxury resort designed to look like an old Ottoman village.

Madaba
LUXURY
Ma'in Spa Hotel, at the Zarqa Ma'in Hot Springs, tel: 03 324

Madaba and the Dead Sea at a Glance

5500, www.sixsenses.com/
Evason-Ma-In/ This hotel
has all the top-end facilities,
including a swimming pool,
indoor heated pool, sauna
and gymnasium. A full range
of health treatments like massage, hydro and mud therapy
are also available at the
health clinic.

BUDGET
Mariam Hotel,
Aisha Umm al-Mumeneen
Street, tel: 05 325 1529,
www.mariamhotel.com
This family-run hotel is the
finest accommodation available in Madaba and the best
in its class in Jordan. It's
clean, cheerful and friendly
with an open-air pool,
restaurant and bar. Charl
al-Twal, the owner, will
arrange discount taxis, tours
and hire cars for you, and
even pick you up from the
airport for a small fee. His
knowledge of local history
is encyclopaedic.
Moab Land Hotel,
just opposite the main
entrance to St George's
Church, tel: 05 325 1318.
Friendly, family-run hotel
opposite the Church of the
Map. Breakfast with a view
on the rooftop terrace.

WHERE TO EAT

Al-Saraya Restaurant,
Mövenpick Resort & Spa
Dead Sea, tel: 05 356 1111.
All-day dining specializing in
international and local dishes.

Ashur Pizza & Grill, Kempinski
Hotel Ishtar Dead Sea, tel: 05
356 8888. The food, with a
strong Mediterranean flavour,
is superb and the ambience
makes this a great place to eat.
Nothing can be more romantic
than dining by the shore of the
Dead Sea as the sun sets over
the West Bank and the lights
of Jericho come on.
Haret J'doudna, just south
of the Church of the Map,
Madaba, tel: 05 324 8650,
www.haretjdoudna.com An
old Ottoman building housing
a superb restaurant. Try a selection of their cold mezes for
lunch. Booking is essential for
dinner on Thursday and Friday.

TOURS AND EXCURSIONS

Jordan Circle Tours, Jebel
Amman, Al-Hayyek Street
(opposite Housing Bank),
Amman, tel: 06 464 3017,
www.jct.com.jo

Abercrombie & Kent Jordan,
Abdullah Bin Abbas Street
(opposite Orchid's Hotel),
Amman, tel: 06 566 5465,
www.akdmc.com
Al-Thuraya Travel & Tours,
PO Box 1883, Amman
11821, tel: 06 553 5525,
www.althurayatravel.net
Jordan Tracks, PO Box 468,
Aqaba, tel: 7964 82801, www.
jordantracks.com Saleem Ali
and his family operate the only
Bedouin-owned tourist agency
in Jordan, based in Wadi Rum.
They also organize tours and
excursions throughout Jordan.

USEFUL CONTACTS

Emergency calls,
tel: 196.
British Embassy,
tel: 06 590 9200.
US Embassy,
tel: 06 590 6000.
Al-Khalidi Medical Centre,
tel: 06 464 4281.

MADABA	J	F	M	A	M	J	J	A	S	O	N	D
AVERAGE TEMP. °F	55	57	66	73	82	86	91	91	86	79	68	59
AVERAGE TEMP. °C	13	14	19	23	28	30	33	33	30	26	20	15
RAINFALL in	1.6	1.2	0.8	2.4	0	0	0	0	0	0.4	0.8	1.6
RAINFALL mm	40	30	20	60	0	0	0	0	0	10	20	40
DAYS OF RAINFALL	2	2	1	1	0	0	0	0	0	1	1	2

AS SAFI	J	F	M	A	M	J	J	A	S	O	N	D
AVERAGE TEMP. °F	70	70	77	86	95	100	105	104	99	90	81	72
AVERAGE TEMP. °C	21	21	25	30	35	38	41	40	37	32	27	22
RAINFALL in	0.8	3.2	3.2	1.6	0	0	0	0	0	0.4	0.4	0.8
RAINFALL mm	20	80	80	40	0	0	0	0	0	10	10	20
DAYS OF RAINFALL	1	1	1	1	0	0	0	0	0	1	1	1

6
The King's Highway

This ancient route is the world's oldest continually used road and has been in existence since prehistoric times. The Patriarch Abraham would have travelled along it on his journey from Mesopotamia to Canaan, although there is no mention of this in the **Bible**. It is first mentioned (Numbers 20:17) during the Exodus of the Children of Israel from Egypt. Moses requested permission from the King of Edom to 'go along the King's Highway' in what is now southern Jordan, but his request was refused.

It started at Heliopolis in Egypt, then crossed the Sinai desert to Eilat and Aqaba before turning north and running along the Great Rift Valley past Petra and Ash Shawback, then through Al-Karak, Madaba, Philadelphia (modern Amman), Jerash and Damascus, before ending at Resafa on the river Euphrates.

It was a major trade route under the **Nabateans** and featured prominently in the transportation of spices and frankincense from Arabia. It was also an important route for pilgrims. **Christians** used it to visit Mount Nebo, and until the 16th century it was the main route for the annual Hajj pilgrimage to **Mecca**.

Most travellers today only journey along short stretches of it, preferring to use the modern **Desert Highway** to move quickly between north and south. While that is a good way to see a lot of Jordan in a limited time, a two- to three-day trip along the King's Highway at a considerably slower pace is a much more satisfactory way to visit some of the country's most important historical attractions.

DON'T MISS

*** **Church of St Stephen:** this World Heritage site at Umm ar-Rasas has breathtaking floor mosaics.
*** **Machaerus:** where Salomé danced and John the Baptist lost his head.
*** **Karak Castle:** one of the most complete and impressive Crusader castles in the Middle East.
*** **Dana Nature Reserve:** wild Jordan at its very best; walking, wildlife, conservation and the preservation of an old way of life.

Opposite: *One of the many breathtaking views seen while hiking in the Dana Nature Reserve.*

Right: *Machaerus fortress was built on top of this hilltop by Herod the Great. It was here that John the Baptist was beheaded.*

Mukawir *

Herod the Great's ancient fortress of **Machaerus** sits on a hilltop beside the village of Mukawir. It was here that **Herod Antipas** imprisoned **John the Baptist** for accusing him of unlawful behaviour for taking his brother's wife, Herodias. On Herod's birthday, Herodias's daughter, **Salomé**, danced for him 'whereupon he promised with an oath to give her whatsoever she would ask'. And Salomé, 'being before instructed of her mother, said, "Give me here John Baptist's head in a charger".' Herod did not want to kill John because 'he feared the multitude, because they counted him as a prophet'. However, an oath sworn in front of his guests was another matter so he ordered John to be beheaded in prison. 'And his head was brought in a charger, and given to the damsel: and she brought it to her mother.'

Just beyond the village is a car park and from there a path and stone steps lead to the **ruined fort** on top of a 700m (2297ft) hill. It was constructed around 100BCE and expanded by **Herod the Great**. Although partially excavated, the ruins are little more than an outline but the steep climb up the steps is well rewarded with the incredible panoramic view from the top. On a clear day

---

EDOM

The Kingdom of Edom occupied what is now southern Jordan and part of the Sinai Peninsula. It was bounded in the north by the Kingdom of Moab and in the south by the Red Sea. Edom was another name given to Esau, and the Edomites are supposedly descended from him. The Kingdom of Edom occupied this region from the 11th century BCE until the time of the Great Jewish Revolt of 66CE.

you will see across the Dead Sea to the occupied Palestinian Territories of the West Bank. At night the lights of Jericho and Jerusalem are clearly visible. Mukawir is about 40km (25 miles) southwest of **Madaba**. To get there, go south to **Libb**, then turn right and continue on the road until it ends in front of Machaerus.

Bani Hamida Textiles *

The Bani Hamida are a Bedouin tribe who live in the mountains of the Dead Sea area. Although the area is impoverished, the lot of the Bedouin women has been greatly improved by the Bani Hamida weaving project. This was initiated in 1985 and, with support from the Queen Noor Foundation and Save the Children's Fund, has grown into a reasonable sized cottage industry. Over a thousand Bedouin women are involved in the work, which involves weaving rugs from locally produced and dyed wool.

Although most of the women work from their own homes, using primitive ground looms built from sticks and stones, others can be found in small centres based in villages. At the main centre in Mukawir visitors can watch the various stages of producing Bani Hamida textiles, and there's a small shop selling the finished product. Rugs can also be bought from the Jordan River Foundation showroom on **Jebel Amman** in Amman.

Al-Karak ***

Al-Karak is just 142km (88 miles) south of Madaba, but on the King's Highway that can be a longish drive. If you are short of time, head south on the Desert Highway and turn right at **Al-Qatrana**. If time is not a problem, the

Below: *A Bedouin woman weaving on a hand loom at the Bani Hamida centre in Mukawir.*

Above: *Karak Castle was built by the Crusaders under King Baldwin I.*

THE MUJIB DAM

In a country short of water this ambitious engineering project was initiated to collect the water from Wadi al-Mujib, Wadi al-Wala and Wadi al-Hasa. The stored water will provide irrigation in the southern Ghors, drinking water for Amman, supply the potash industry and allow expansion of tourism on the Dead Sea. Completed in December 2003, it took four years to build. The King's Highway has been diverted to cross over the dam. The best views are to be had from the terrace of the restaurant at the top of the gorge south of the wadi.

---

scenic route is much nicer and involves crossing the **Wadi al-Mujib** – one of the most spectacular sights in Jordan. In biblical times this was the **Arnon** mentioned in Judges 11:18. It's a 1000m (3281ft) deep gorge which formed the natural boundary separating the kingdoms of the Moabites and the Amorites.

Al-Karak was the capital of Moab. Standing 1000m (3281ft) above the Dead Sea valley and with a commanding view of the surrounding countryside, it was of great strategic importance. The main caravan routes from Syria to Egypt passed through the town and it later became an important citadel for the Greeks and Romans. They called it **Characmoba** and it has also been known as **Qir Heres**, **Qir Moab** and **Hareseth**.

It was the arrival of the **Crusaders** in the 12th century that enabled it to reach its true potential. The castle was built on the orders of **King Baldwin I** of Jerusalem in 1132. It formed a vital link in the line of Crusader castles stretching from Aqaba to Turkey. Midway between Jerusalem and Ash Shawbak, it became the capital of the Crusader district of **Oultrejourdain**, collecting taxes from the surrounding countryside and passing caravans.

In the late 13th century the Mamelukes rebuilt the castle and it has now been partially restored. It is one of the most spectacular buildings in Jordan. Visitors can wander through a maze of vaulted passages and explore the rooms. To the right of the entrance a series of stone stairs leads to the **museum** with its collection of Mameluke pottery, some Nabatean and Roman coins, and a copy of the famous **Mesha Stele**. Open daily, 08:00–19:00 (April–September) and 08:00–16:00 (October–March); admission JD1.

King's Highway

Khirbet al-Tannur *

Continuing south on the King's Highway from Al-Karak another deep gorge, **Wadi al-Hasa**, is crossed. This was the biblical **Zered Valley** where **Moses** and the **Israelites** camped on their journey north (Numbers 21:12; Deuteronomy 2:13–14).

Just west of the gorge is **Khirbet al-Tannur**, the ruins of a Nabatean temple dating back to the 1st century CE. Although excavations have unearthed artefacts associated with several Nabatean gods, archaeologists believe it was dedicated to **Atargatis**, the goddess of foliage and fruit, and the god of the thunderbolt, **Hadad**. Most of the artefacts recovered from the temple are on display in **Amman Museum**.

Tafila Crusader Fortress *

The town of At Tafila, south of Wadi al-Hasa, is a small but busy market town. During the **Crusades**, it was an important link in the Crusaders' defences and the ruins of their long abandoned **fortress** remain to be explored. It was here, during the Arab revolt, that **Lawrence of Arabia** fought his only set battle and defeated a vastly superior force of Turks. The country between here and Shawbak once had **rich metal deposits**. In biblical times the Edomites developed copper mining and smelting and grew very wealthy as a result.

Dana Nature Reserve ***

Dana is an idyllic mountain village with a superb view along the Wadi al-Dana. The people who occupied this small cluster of stone-built Ottoman cottages lived a

RAYNOD DE CHATILLON

The governor of Al-Karak was a particularly offensive individual who threw Muslim captives from the battlements. First he encased their heads in wooden boxes so that they would remain fully conscious until they hit the ground. He broke a truce between Salah al-Din and the Crusader King by raiding a caravan of pilgrims taking part in the Hajj to Mecca. Salah al-Din besieged Karak, eventually taking it and capturing De Chatillon whom he personally beheaded.

Opposite: *Some of the women of Dana have become skilled jewellers.*
Below: *The terrace of the Trajan rest house is an ideal spot to stop for coffee or lunch.*

simple **agricultural life** until well into the 20th century. Then encroaching modernization and increasing living standards led to a gradual decline. When a **cement factory** was built nearby, villagers deserted the land in droves, forsaking the uncertainty of agriculture for a regular weekly wage. Most of them settled in the new village of **Al-Qadisiyya** and Dana was left to decay. Eventually it would have been reduced to just some small piles of stones of interest only to historians and archaeologists, had not a group calling themselves the '**Friends of Dana**' intervened.

In the late 1990s, working under the banner of the **Royal Society for the Conservation of Nature**, they instigated a project aimed at reversing the decline. The old buildings were renovated and modernized. A new water system was built, electricity and telephone lines installed and gradually the people have been persuaded to return.

But providing improved accommodation on its own was not enough to resurrect a community, so the 'Friends' turned their attention to ways of revitalizing the agriculture. New sustainable practices were introduced. Then projects were initiated to process the crops. By

adding value to the produce, the 'Friends' were able to help maximize the income villagers could receive from agriculture. Only then could it compete with the lure of the cement factory.

Dana village is now almost self-sufficient. **Ecotourism** and **workshops** help to support the community and the conservation work in the reserve. Most of the **craft** production, including silver jewellery and pottery, is done by the women while the men work as rangers, tour guides, cooks, cleaners, shop and camp-site managers and receptionists. They grow their own fruit and vegetables in the terraced **organic gardens** that surround the village. Some of this is processed into dried fruit and herbs and organic food and snacks.

Dana offers a wealth of activities for visitors. If time is short a simple stroll through the village and the terraced gardens is sure to whet the appetite for a return visit. People with a few days to

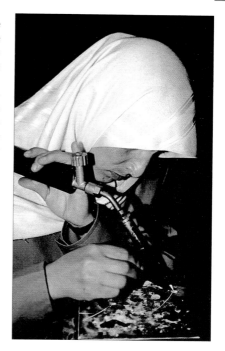

stay can enjoy the spectacular view along the wadi from the terrace of the **Government Rest House**. Or they can elect to stay in the Dana Co-operative Hotel or on one of the camp sites in the wadi, explore archaeological sites, hike through several regions of the reserve, and visit the workshops and gift shop.

Wadi al-Feynan ★★★

A few years ago this remote part of Dana Nature reserve was home to a handful of **Bedouins** eking out a subsistence existence herding goats. Unfortunately the goats were endangering the fragile ecosystem and some of the rare plants that grew there. To combat this and reduce the Bedouins' dependency on goats, the **Royal Society for the Conservation of Nature** initiated a leather-working project. Bedouin women were trained

THE CRUSADES

This was a series of military operations, sanctioned by various popes, that date from 1095 to 1291CE. The Crusades resulted in hordes of armed warriors from Christian Europe invaded the Levant with the aim of recapturing Jerusalem and liberating the 'Holy Land' from Muslim rule. For this they were promised remission of sin. Most Crusaders believed that by capturing Jerusalem in a just and holy war they would go immediately to heaven when they died.

Above: *Wadi al-Feynan Eco Lodge is solar powered by day and in the evening lit by candles made in its candle workshop.*

ROYAL SOCIETY FOR THE CONSERVATION OF NATURE

This is a voluntary conservation organization created in 1966 under the patronage of Queen Noor. The late King Hussein was its honorary president. It exists to safeguard and preserve Jordan's wildlife and scenic areas, promote the use of natural resources, and help the development of rural communities. It has established protected reserves at Ajloun, Azraq, Dana, Shaumari, Wadi Mujib and Wadi Rum and has reintroduced a number of animal species, including the Arabian oryx, into the wild.

to cure goat skins and make a variety of craft products from them. In its early days the women worked outside under a crudely constructed shade. Now they have premises, are selling their products in the Society's shops and are prospering.

The Society have expanded their activities in Wadi al-Feynan and in the summer of 2005 opened an **Eco Lodge**. Using readily available materials and a local architect they have built an eco-friendly lodge to a unique arabesque design. It incorporates traditional adobe building techniques and blends totally with its surroundings. By day it is powered by solar energy and at night is lit by candles produced by the Bedouin women in the candle workshop, another RSCN project.

The lodge was built as a base for visitors who want to explore the area on foot or mountain bike and is not the easiest of places to reach. A longish drive in from the Dead Sea Highway takes you to reception in the nearest village. From there it is another half-hour on a very rocky and bumpy road in a truck belonging to one of the Bedouins.

While the accommodation is excellent and the food splendid, people are attracted to Feynan for its atmosphere and to explore this remote corner of Dana. Take a guided walk through the desert to visit **copper mines** that have been deserted since the Romans departed, do your own thing walking or biking the unmarked local trails, or join a trek along several long-distance routes. Choices include walking north along the wadi to Dana village and heading south on the trail to Petra.

Shawbak Crusader Fortress ★★★

This is probably the most spectacular of Jordan's Crusader castles, mainly because it is not surrounded by other buildings. It sits on top of a small hill 2km (1.2 miles) northeast of Shawbak town and can be reached by turning off the King's Highway and heading west for 4km (2.5 miles).

This was the Crusaders' **Montreal (Mont Realis)**, built in 1115 by **King Baldwin I**. At its peak some 6000 people lived here. Like Al-Karak it was besieged several times by **Salah al-Din**, who finally took it in 1189.

There are two **churches** within the fortress, as well as ruins of **baths**, **cisterns** and **rainwater pipes**. A shaft leads to a set of 375 steps cut into the rocks to the deepest well ever built by the Crusaders. This was one of the reasons why the fortress was able to withstand so many sieges. The caretaker is an interesting character and is happy to pose for photographs on the ramparts. Naturally, he will appreciate a small payment.

UMM AR-RASAS

The third of Jordan's World Heritage sites lies a few miles east of the King's Highway beyond Dhiban. This former Roman camp contains remains from the Roman period, as well as the Byzantine and early Muslim periods. Very little excavation has been done but the **Church of St Stephen**, with its well-preserved mosaic floors, is a must-see. Nearby, two square towers would once have been used by Stylite monks for their solitary meditation.

Below: *Shawbak, the most spectacular of Jordan's Crusader castles, sits sentinel-like on the top of a hill.*

The Kings Highway at a Glance

Spring (March–May) and autumn (September–October) are the best times to visit. The days are temperate at around 25–30°C (77–86°F). The nights are chilly year-round. In summer the days are extremely hot, while in winter days and nights are cold.

Travelling the King's Highway is one of the great road journeys of the world. Unfortunately public transport is almost non-existent so the only way to do the whole trip is by self-drive car. Buses go from Amman to Al-Karak, At Tafila and Ash Shawbak, but along the Desert Highway, and there is not one that visits all three places in turn.

The only satisfactory way to explore the King's Highway is by self-drive car. Charl al-Twal at the Mariam Hotel in Madaba can organize a trip to Petra along the King's Highway.

Amman
LUXURY
Kempinski, Abdul Hameed Shouman Street, Shmeisani, PO Box 941045, Amman, 11194, tel: 06 520 0200, www.kempinski-amman.com Unashamed luxury with fine dining and splendid views. One of the best hotels in the city centre.

Le Meridien, Queen Noor Street, Shmeisani, PO Box 950629, Amman, 11195, tel: 06 569 6511, www.starwood hotels.com/lemeridien/ property/overview/index. html?propertyID=1878 Another world-class hotel in the heart of the city, with a choice of international cuisine including food from Lebanon, Japan and Mongolia.

Dead Sea
LUXURY
Kempinski Hotel Ishtar Dead Sea, Dead Sea Road, PO Box 815554, Amman 11180, tel: 05 356 8888, www.kempinski. com/en/deadsea Without a doubt this is *the* most luxurious hotel in Jordan. It was designed in tribute to the Hanging Gardens of Babylon and draws heavily on Sumerian architecture.
Jordan Valley Marriott Resort and Spa, Dead Sea Road, Sweimeh, tel : 05 356 0400, www.marriott.co.uk/hotels/ travel/qmdjv-jordan-valley-marriott-resort-and-spa/ Grand luxury hotel on the shores of the Dead Sea with fine views and spectacular sunsets over the West Bank. The spa offers a series of upscale treatments using the natural elements of the Dead Sea.

Madaba
LUXURY
Ma'in Spa Hotel, at the Zarqa Ma'in Hot Springs, tel: 03 324 5500, www.sixsenses.com/

Evason-Ma-In/ The hotel has top-end facilities, including a swimming pool, indoor heated pool, sauna and gymnasium. A full range of health treatments like massage, hydro and mud therapy are also available at the health clinic.

BUDGET
Mariam Hotel, Aisha Umm al-Mumeneen Street, Madaba, tel: 05 325 1529, www.mariamhotel.com This family-run hotel is the finest accommodation available in Madaba and the best in its class in Jordan. It's clean, cheerful and friendly, with an open-air pool, restaurant and bar. Charl al-Twal, the owner, will arrange discount taxis, tours and hire cars, and even pick you up from the airport for a small fee. His knowledge of local history is encyclopaedic.

Al-Karak
BUDGET
Mujeb Alsyahi Hotel, just outside Al-Karak at the junction of the King's Highway and Desert Highway, tel: 03 238 6090. A popular, but basic, tourist hotel with clean, *en-suite* rooms and pretty decent food.
Al-Kamah, Al-Karak Downtown, tel: 03 235 1942. Very basic, but the place to head for if money is tight.
Karak Rest House, near the entrance to the Castle, tel: 03 235 1148. Government-run

rest house providing simple but clean accommodation at a reasonable price.

Towers Hotel, tel: 03 235 4293. A stone's throw from the castle entrance, this is a decent budget hotel. Facilities are very basic but the staff are friendly and the service good.

Dana Village
BUDGET
Dana Tower Hotel, Dana Village, tel: 02 795 688 853, www.danatowerhotel.com This is a decent alternative to the Guest House (see below). It also has a superb view.

SPECIAL HOTELS
Dana Guest House, Dana Village, tel: 06 464 5580. This is run by the RSCN and is more expensive than government rest houses. But the atmosphere is fantastic. The view from the terrace and each of the rooms is along the length of the Wadi Dana. At night the silence is incredible. With only nine rooms, this needs to be booked well in advance.

Wadi al-Feynan Eco Lodge, Wadi al-Feynan, access to reception is from the Dead Sea Highway, tel: 06 464 5580, www.feynan.com This is another RSCN establishment. This one is in the Wadi al-Feynan and is a half-hour truck ride from the reception in the nearest village. Solar powered by day and lit at night from candles made by the Bedouin women on the premises, this

is as good as it gets in terms of a 'get away from it all' place.

Rummana Campsite, Dana Reserve, near Dana Village, tel: 06 464 5580. Advance booking is essential and all equipment including tents is provided. It has good toilets, cold-water showers and a self-catering kitchen. For groups of six or more, arrangements can be made for staff to prepare food. A night spent sleeping under canvas on the reserve is an experience unlikely ever to be forgotten.

WHERE TO EAT

Al-Karak
Avoid the touristy establishments near the castle and instead head downtown and try any of the little diners that take your fancy. Simple, well-cooked Bedouin food is on offer at unbelievably low prices.

Dana Village
There are no restaurants and all meals are provided by the hotels.

Wadi al-Feynan
Wadi al-Feynan Eco Lodge, (see Where to Stay). Simple

Arab fare superbly cooked by local Bedouin.

TOURS AND EXCURSIONS

Jordan Circle Tours, Jebel Amman, Al-Hayyek Street (opposite Housing Bank), Amman, tel: 06 464 3017, www.jct.com.jo
Abercrombie & Kent Jordan, Abdullah Bin Abbas Street (opposite Orchid's Hotel), Amman, tel: 06 566 5465, www.akdmc.com
Al-Thuraya Travel & Tours, PO Box 1883, Amman 11821, tel: 06 553 5525, www.althurayatravel.net
Jordan Tracks, PO Box 468, Aqaba, tel: 7964 82801, www.jordantracks.com
Saleem Ali and his family operate the only Bedouin-owned tourist agency in Jordan, based in Wadi Rum. They also organize tours and excursions throughout Jordan.

USEFUL CONTACTS

Emergency calls, tel: 196.
British Embassy, tel: 06 590 9200.
US Embassy, tel: 06 590 6000.
Al-Khalidi Medical Centre, tel: 06 464 4281.

AT TAFILA	J	F	M	A	M	J	J	A	S	O	N	D
AVERAGE TEMP. °F	52	54	59	70	80	86	88	88	86	79	66	54
AVERAGE TEMP. °C	11	12	15	21	27	30	31	31	30	26	19	12
RAINFALL in	2.4	0.8	1.2	3.6	0.4	0	0	0	0	0.8	0.6	1
RAINFALL mm	60	20	30	90	10	0	0	0	0	20	15	25
DAYS OF RAINFALL	5	2	3	1	1	0	0	0	0	1	1	3

7
Petra

Petra is the most famous attraction in Jordan, no mean feat in a country steeped in history. It means 'stone' in Greek, an apt title as most of the buildings have been carved by hand from the sandstone of a deep canyon on the edge of the **Wadi Araba**.

It was listed as a **UNESCO World Heritage site** in 1985 and although no one can say for certain when it was founded, archaeologists think it may have been as early as the 5th century BCE.

The city was created by the **Nabateans**, a great trading race of Arabic-speaking Semitics who moved into southern Jordan from the **Arabian Peninsula** two thousand years ago. From their capital at Petra they controlled the trade routes stretching from Africa to India and China. They grew rich levying tolls and offering shelter and protection to caravans laden with ivory and hides, silks and spices, and frankincense and myrrh.

Petra's decline started after the **Romans** conquered the area, mainly due to a change in trading routes. The population dropped and earthquakes caused damage to the buildings and water-storage system. Eventually ruined and abandoned, it was forgotten until the Swiss traveller **Johann Ludwig Burchhardt** rediscovered it in 1812.

Getting into Petra is almost as exciting as the city itself. Access is through **the Siq**, a narrow gorge twisting and turning through the rock. You can make the journey by horse or horse-drawn carriage but it is best walked to get the full atmospheric effect and to take the time to look at all the geological formations, colourful

DON'T MISS

*** Al-Khazneh (The Treasury): first and most spectacular of Petra's buildings.
*** The Monastery: bigger than the Treasury and built on a mountaintop site, this is well worth the long climb.
** Qasr el Bint al-Faroun: the only free-standing building to have survived the earthquakes that destroyed everything else.
** The Urn Tomb: the largest tomb and one that was also used as a Byzantine church.
* The Silk Tomb: the most colourful building in Petra.

Opposite: *Tourists walking through the Siq, the only entrance to Petra.*

rocks, water channels, and votive niches carved into the rock. As you near the end you know exactly what you are going to see. After all, you've seen it in the film *Indiana Jones and the Last Crusade*, on tourism posters, and there's even a photograph in this book (*see* page 4). But none of these will have prepared you for the reality. As you turn round the last bend and catch your first glimpse of **Al-Khazneh**, you may well imagine that you've been transported back through time to the centuries preceding the birth of Christ.

Al-Khazneh (The Treasury) ★★★

This is undoubtedly the most beautiful monument here and of an architectural style unique in the ancient world. The design of the façade was influenced by Alexandrian Hellenistic architecture but adapted to the style of the **Nabatean** craftsmen who painstakingly chiselled it from solid stone. It was completed some time in the century before Christ's birth as a tomb for an important Nabatean king and later may have served as a temple. The inside is a stark contrast to the ornate exterior and is not very large. There are no extensive caverns, no hidden traps to behead the unwary nor an ancient Crusader guarding the Holy Grail. That, I'm afraid, was just a movie set.

Below: *The Theatre in Petra is carved into the solid rock and, although it looks Roman, was actually built by the Nabateans and then enlarged by the Romans.*

Street of Façades ★★★

This is reached by passing the Treasury and heading along the **Outer Siq**. The façades are the tombs of prominent Nabateans. Rows of them remain in various states of preservation and it is still possible to see the intricacy of the carvings.

'Roman' Theatre ★★

Near the end of the Street of Façades is a theatre that looks Roman. It's not. It was built by the Nabateans in the 1st century CE when Jordan was already under Roman rule. It's no surprise that the Nabatean builders borrowed a Roman design. Very little of this theatre is freestanding. Like the rest of Petra, it is mostly carved into the rock. When it was new it could seat 7000 people.

Royal Tombs ★★★

A short distance further, a path leads off to the right and heads uphill towards what are known as the **Royal Tombs**. Once they rivalled the Treasury in their ornate carvings but now are badly eroded. They housed the tombs of Nabatean nobles.

Above: *The Street of Façades contains tombs of prominent Nabateans and their elaborate carvings are still visible.*

PETRA POEM

'Match me such a marvel save in Eastern clime, A rose-red city half as old as time.'
John William Burgon's poetic description of this legendary city is spot-on, even if he did write it 16 years before his own visit. But he lived in a time when Victorian travellers were returning with tales of this fabled city and he would have known what it looked like from the art of the time.

THE NABATEANS

This race of nomadic traders started arriving in what is now southern Jordan from Arabia during the 6th century BCE. They settled at Petra and made it their capital. They became skilled in water preservation and used their reservoirs to help them control the trading routes. Their origins are obscure but they may have been descended from the Nebaioth tribe recorded in Genesis. Initially they spoke Arabic but later changed to Aramaic.

Below: *The Nabateans were masters of water preservation, storage and irrigation. This is one of their systems for carrying water through the Siq.*

The first one is the **Urn Tomb** and it is the largest of them all. It was constructed around 70CE and may have been the tomb of **Malchus II** who died at that time. It has an immense courtyard and a very large chamber. Three other chambers can be seen above the doorway. The courtyard originally extended much further out and would have been supported by arches, the remains of which are visible. High up on top of the pediment is the carved urn which has given this tomb its modern name. Considerable alterations in the mid-5th century converted the tomb for use as a **Byzantine church**. Next to it the **Silk Tomb** has the most colourful façade of any of the buildings in Petra.

The **Corinthian Tomb** got its name because early writers mistakenly thought that the carved pillars were Corinthian, but they are actually just variations of the ones on the Treasury. Fallen rocks and tens of hundreds of years of erosion have exacted a heavy toll on this building but it is still possible to see that the upper part is almost a replica of the more famous Treasury.

The **Palace Tomb** looks like a palace. It stands on a carved platform and is one of the widest monuments in proportion to its height. There are three levels richly adorned with pillars and decorations.

There is only a single monument in the whole of Petra that can be accurately described – the **Tomb of Sextius Florentius**. It was built for the Roman Governor of the Province of Arabia and there is a carved inscription saying so. Sextius Florentius wanted to be buried in Petra but it was not he who had the tomb built. According

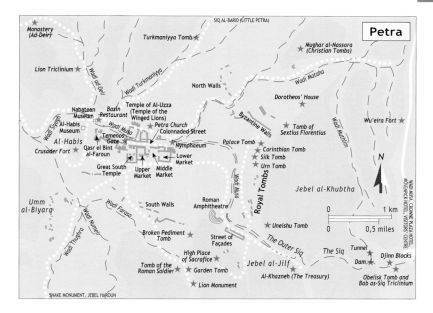

to the inscription it was his son who had it carved. Sextius Florentius was Governer in 127CE but had been succeeded by Haterius Nepos by 130CE. So it can be assumed that the tomb was constructed sometime between 127 and 131. Although built during the Roman period, the design is still heavily influenced by Nabatean architecture.

You can follow the path round from these tombs and continue on steps cut into the stone that climb up the side of a chasm, twisting and turning to reach the top. As well as superb views over most of Petra, this is a great spot for taking outstanding photographs. It is possible to continue from here along a faint dirt and rock path to reach the cliff top looking down onto the Treasury building, but this is best done with a guide.

The Nymphaeum ★

Not much remains of the **Nymphaeum** which lies not far from the Theatre near the start of the Colonnaded

---

JOHANN LUDWIG BURCKHARDT

Burckhardt was a Swiss explorer and orientalist who had a short but brilliant life. After studying Arabic at Cambridge University he left for the Levant to improve his language and master Islamic law. Disguised as a Muslim and calling himself Sheikh Ibrahim Ibn Abdallah, he travelled throughout the Middle East, even making the pilgrimage to Mecca. On one of his trips in 1812 he discovered the lost city of Petra. He died of dysentery in Cairo aged 33.

Above: *The Temenos Gate, one of Petra's few free-standing monuments, was once the entrance to a sacred complex.*

Street. Only the foundations remain of the once ornate public fountain, which was a large building with a recessed half-dome. The **Colonnaded Street** has more in the way of remains, with several columns re-erected and also the remains of a marble pavement. This was the main street leading into the city centre and it was flanked by shops, public buildings and temples. All around, the hillsides were crowded with houses that were destroyed during the great earthquakes.

The Markets ★★

On the left side of the Colonnaded Street a flight of wide steps leads up to what was once the **Upper Market**. That in turn opened into the **Middle** and **Lower Markets**. This flat area has not yet been excavated but beyond it is the **Great South Temple** where archaeologists from Brown University in the USA have been working since 1993. If you visit during the season you will be able to watch them work. It's a painstaking business but gradually they are beginning to uncover the building and have begun reconstruction work.

Temple of Al-Uzza ★

Opposite here, on the hillside at the other side of the street, is the **Temple of Al-Uzza** or **Temple of the Winged Lions** where excavations have been ongoing since the 1970s. A painter's workshop was unearthed in a side room off the temple. It was full of pottery vessels containing the pigment used in the decoration

---

AARON

The brother of Moses and Priest of Israel is also revered by Muslims as the Prophet Harun bin Imran, descendant of the Prophet Ibrahim/ Abraham through his grandson Jacob. Like his brother Moses, he was not permitted to enter the promised land of Canaan. He died on the summit of Mount Hor near Petra and his tomb is in the highest of its two peaks. A small domed mosque has been built over the tomb.

of the building. The approach to the temple was by a series of ascending terraces which started from a bridge over the wadi, but little of that remains.

The Temenos Gate ★★

Situated at the end of the Colonnaded Street is one of the few original free-standing monuments that survived the earthquakes in Petra. The **Temenos Gate** once had heavy wooden doors that could be closed and barred. Sockets for the bolts and hinges and a curb running across the central opening show where they once were. This was the entrance to a sacred complex containing the main temple of the Nabatean capital, the **Qasr el Bint al-Faroun**.

Qasr el Bint al-Faroun ★★★

In Arabic this means 'the house of the daughter of the Pharaoh'. Excavations unearthed a Nabatean inscription, 'Su'udat, daughter of Maliku', referring to the daughter of Malchus II, a local king.

Built around the 1st century BCE it is another free-standing construction in Petra to have survived. It was a colossal building standing on a podium with steps running its full width to the portico of the main entrance.

Four great pillars supported the portico which was topped by a classical pediment. All that remain are the stumps of the pillars and beyond them the entrance arch of the main door. The temple was decorated inside and out with painted plasterwork, and to the front of the entrance a marble-clad outdoor altar platform was used for religious ceremonies.

The principal Nabatean god was **Dushara**, meaning

> ### DEHYDRATION
>
> Petra can get very hot, particularly at the height of summer, and dehydration is a serious risk. Water and soft drinks are plentiful in the main part of the city. However, if you intend to go a bit off the beaten track to visit the Monastery, High Place of Sacrifice or head back along the cliff top to get that spectacular photograph of the Treasury, make sure you have plenty of water with you.

Below: *This is an ancient statue, carved out of the sandstone in the Siq, of a man leading a camel. Although badly eroded, the outline is still clear.*

Below: *The long trek up to the Monastery is much easier on a donkey.*

'He of Shara', referring to the Shara Mountains. As the temple faces north towards these mountains it has been assumed that it was dedicated to that god. It remained in use well into the Roman period but was apparently looted and set on fire. This destroyed the roof and most of the interior. The earthquake of 363CE brought down most of the walls, rendering it unusable.

Immediately opposite the Qasr el Bint al-Faroun is the **Basin Restaurant** where you can enjoy some shade and get a drink or some food. Petra's **museum** is also here and it is worth spending some time in it. Petra's geography and history is covered in depth, as is the story of the Nabateans. There are interpretation boards and displays of artefacts uncovered in the city and surrounding area from as far back as the Neolithic period. The displays include pottery, coins, statues, jewellery and the stone idol from the Temple of the Winged Lion. The museum is open daily, 09:00–16:00.

Most tours allow half a day or a day at the most. You could easily spend four or five days exploring this city and still not see everything. If you have the time, buy a multi-day ticket and get here when it opens. You'll miss the crowds, and the early morning light will produce the best photographs. Similarly, later in the afternoon when the tour buses have gone it is much quieter and the setting sun bathes the red sandstone in an almost orange glow.

The Monastery ★★★

From the museum there's a path and a flight of 800 steps cut from the rock that will take you on a steep climb, twisting and turning up through a narrowing gorge, to **Ad-Deir** on the top of a mountain. This, the second most famed building in Petra, is also known as **The Monastery**. Afternoon is the best time to visit here, when the sun bathes the façade with light.

In design it is similar to the Treasury but a bit shorter and much broader and has less in the way of decoration. It may have been a temple or a tomb or even both. Inside there is just one large plain chamber. The ground in front of the building has been levelled, indicating perhaps that crowds once gathered here during important rituals. A short walk across here will take you to the edge of the plateau overlooking the **Wadi Araba** with views across to **Jebel Haroun** and the shrine of the **Prophet Aaron**.

You really will have to spend some time here and be pretty fit to make the hard climb up the long flights of stone steps to the **High Place of Sacrifice**. This was an important place for rituals and ceremonies honouring the Nabatean gods. It's also one of the best-preserved sacred places from biblical times.

A shallow courtyard has been cut out of the rock. Within it is a low stone **Mensa Sacra** or offerings table just before the altar platform. The Nabateans practised human sacrifice here. We know this from an inscription found at Hegra tells us that 'Abd-Wadd, priest of Wadd and his son Salim, and Zayd-Wadd, have consecrated the young man Salim to be immolated to Dhu Gabat.'

Above: *Ad-Deir, or the Monastery, the second most famed building in Petra, sits on a mountain top reached after a rather steep climb.*

TAYBET ZAMAN

Take one ancient and decaying village in the middle of a small town. Add a visionary mayor, some investment and the result is the most imaginative hotel in Jordan. The village could have been flattened and a new hotel built on the site but instead each of the old buildings was lovingly restored to become a suite in this splendid hotel. Elsewhere in Jordan you'll find a late 20th-century hotel just like it. But this is the real deal.

Petra at a Glance

Spring (March–May) and autumn (September–October) are the best times to visit. The days are temperate at around 25–30°C (77–86°F). The nights are chilly year-round. In summer the days are extremely hot, while in winter days and nights are cold. Early morning and late afternoon are the best times to see Petra at its best, with the rocks glowing red in the sun.

From Amman: Modern air-conditioned coaches depart from Abdali station. For details, contact JETT, tel: 06 566 4146. Minibuses run from Wahedat station to Petra every two hours except on Friday when there may be none in the afternoon.
By car, Petra is a well-signposted three-hour drive on the Desert Highway.
From Aqaba: Minibuses run from Aqaba every day but they are infrequent and irregular. (There is also a minibus from Wadi Rum and one from Karak.)

If you have no car, a taxi is the only means of transport. Try Al-Anbat, tel: 03 215 6777, or al-Hilali, tel: 03 215 6600 or pick up a taxi in the street. In Petra itself the only transport is the donkey taxi, well worth taking on some of the steep climbs.

LUXURY
Mövenpick Resort Petra, tel: 03 215 7111, fax: 215 7112, www.movenpick-petra.com Handsome four-star with stunning four-storey courtyard atrium, it is a three-minute walk to the city.
Crowne Plaza Resort, tel (front desk): 962 3215 6266, fax: 962 3215 6977, www.petra.crowneplaza.com This four-star hotel is ideally suited to the business customer, with excellent facilities for off-duty relaxation to enhance your stay.
Golden Tulip Kings Way, Petra, tel: 03 567 9957, fax: 567 9954. A four-star hotel decorated with rose-red Petra colours and traditional embroidery. It is situated on the main road to the city centre, requiring a five-minute taxi ride to the site.
Petra Marriott Hotel, on the Taybeh Road away from the village, tel: 03 215 6407, www.marriott.co.uk/hotels/travel/mpqmc-petra-mariott-hotel This is built on the hillside and has unbelievable views of the mountains of Petra. Sunsets are particularly spectacular when viewed from here. The accommodation is first class, as is the service.

MID-RANGE
The Petra Palace, tel: 03 215 6723, fax 215 6724, www.petrapalace.com.jo/ This comfortable three-star hotel is near the gate to Petra.

Amra Palace, tel: 03 215 7070, fax: 215 7071, www.amrapalace.com The three-star Amra Palace Hotel is located at the heart of the city, in a quiet back street, minutes away from the main shopping areas and the entrance to the ancient city. The hotel is owned and managed by a local family.
Edom, tel: 03 215 6995, fax: 215 6994, www.edomhotel.com/index_e.htm Comfortable three-star; good value for money and worth checking for out of season deals.

BUDGET
The Petra Moon, tel: 777 919 709, fax: 03 215 4547, www.petramoonhotel.com This two-star hotel was one of the few cheaper options close to the entrance to Petra. However, it closed during 2010 for extensive renovations to allow it to update to three stars. Check the website for details.
The Petra Sunset, tel: 03 215 6579, fax: 215 6950, www.petrasunset.com Cheap and close to the entrance but little else to recommend it.
The Alanbat Two, tel: 03 215 6265, fax: 03 215 6888, www.alanbat.com Raja O. Nawafleh and his brothers were the first local family to invest in hotels and services.
The Alanbat One, tel: 03 215 6265, fax: 03 215 6888, www.alanbat.com Situated further up the hill and pleasantly cool in hot weather,

they provide a taxi service to the gate of Petra.

Mussa Spring, tel: 03 215 6310, fax: 215 6910. This is more of a backpackers' hostel than a hotel, but is comfortably equipped, cheap and offers free transport to Petra. As well as rooms it has dormitories for backpackers too, equipped with shared bath and showers, 24-hour hot water and satellite TV.

SPECIAL HOTELS

Taybet Zaman Hotel & Resort, Petra, tel: 03 215 0111, fax: 215 0101. This unique hotel was a 19th-century Jordanian village called Taybeh, now refurbished with all the features of a top-class luxury hotel. The suites are authentic village houses, linked by winding passageways and souks. But because it is a very old building there are uneven floors and walls. Some people do not like this and would prefer the 20th-century copy at the Mövenpick Dead Sea. It is located about 11km south of the ancient city.

WHERE TO EAT

Good eating places are sparse inside Petra so it's a good idea to take a packed lunch and plenty of water to drink.

The Basin, tel: 03 215 6266. This is about the best place to eat inside Petra itself. It is crowded and expensive for what it is, but the food is plain and fresh.

Al Qantarah, off the Petra-Wadi Musa road, 5m from the main gate at Petra, tel: 03 215 5535, mobile: 03 795 645 707, www.al-qantarah.com Run by local people who cook Jordanian food in a traditional taboun – the old-style clay oven that Jordanians use to bake bread and grill meat. You can watch them cook your meal and they will explain the ingredients and techniques used and, if you are lucky, you may be invited to help.

The Red Cave, tel: 03 215 7799. This restaurant is close to the gate and serves a range of traditional dishes. It is large, serves excellent food and the prices are very modest.

Al-Arabi, located in the centre of the village. The food is excellent and cheap. The restaurant serves a range of authentic Arabic dishes, including all sorts of salads with falafel, hummus, kebabs, tabouleh and fresh bread.

Al-Ilwan, tel: 03 215 7111. This is the up-scale restaurant of the Mövenpick Resort (see Where to Stay). Situated in a stunning setting in the atrium of the hotel, the food is classic Arabic superbly presented

and served with sophistication. The prices match the classy setting and service.

TOURS AND EXCURSIONS

Baïda is a beautiful semi-desert area close to Petra. A shuttle bus departs from in front of the main mosque in the village. At Little Petra there are Nabatean cisterns, which still store water in the summer. The nearby Neolithic village dates from 7000BCE. It is possible to hire a guide for the day to explore the surrounding area. Mohammed Hasanat is an experienced guide, who can organize various explorations of the surounding area. Contact him at tel: 0795 603 114, e-mail: explorerone69@yahoo.com

USEFUL CONTACTS

Petra Archaeological Park Visitors Centre, at entrance to site, www.petrapark.com/visitor-center
Ministry of Tourism, Petra, tel: 03 215 6029.
Jordan Tourist Board, Amman, tel: 06 567 8294.
Royal Society for the Conservation of Nature (RSCN), tel: 06 533 7931.

PETRA	J	F	M	A	M	J	J	A	S	O	N	D
AVERAGE TEMP. °F	57	59	70	77	82	90	93	95	90	82	68	59
AVERAGE TEMP. °C	14	15	21	25	28	32	34	35	32	28	20	15
RAINFALL in	0.2	1.2	0.8	0.4	0.2	0	0	0	0	0.8	0.4	0.2
RAINFALL mm	5	30	20	10	5	0	0	0	0	20	10	5
DAYS OF RAINFALL	2	2	2	1	1	0	0	0	0	1	1	2

8. Aqaba & the Southeastern Desert

The south of Jordan is a sparsely populated adventure playground where it is possible to combine a typical beach holiday with some of the finest diving on the planet or get far away from the stresses of the modern world in the vastness of the southern desert.

Aqaba, on the northern tip of the Red Sea, is Jordan's only port and crucial to its economy. In 1965, settlement of a border dispute with Saudi Arabia added a few extra miles of coastline and coral reef to the south of Aqaba. Those crucial few miles transformed Aqaba from a sleepy fishing village into a modern port.

In 2001 King Abdullah declared Aqaba a free trade zone, providing tax breaks on a range of goods and services. That gave visitors the opportunity to pick up a range of duty-free bargains. More importantly, it attracted considerable foreign investment including a number of international hotel chains.

With continual sunshine and with winter temperatures around 25°C (77°F), it is a year-round beach resort and a favourite holiday destination for Jordan's Royal Family. The **Red Sea** provides near perfect diving conditions and there are plenty of opportunities to enjoy wind-surfing, water-skiing, fishing and sailing. With the Israeli resort of Eilat visible a few miles along the beach and Egypt and the Sinai Peninsula just a short ferry ride away, it is hardly surprising that the Gulf of Aqaba is attracting a steadily rising number of cruise liners.

East of Aqaba and the **Desert Highway** running to Amman is a vast, sandy desert that stretches to the

---

Don't Miss

*** Aqaba Fort: a Mameluke fort associated with Lawrence of Arabia.
*** Jordan Experience: a realistic simulation of a flight round Jordan's main attractions.
*** Wadi Rum Desert: backdrop for David Lean's epic film *Lawrence of Arabia*.
*** Bedouin of Wadi Rum: these semi-nomadic desert dwellers uphold an ancient code of hospitality.

Opposite: *The beach resort town of Aqaba is Jordan's only port.*

Above: *Aqaba is a small and compact city that grew up round the remains of the old Islamic city of Ayla (foreground).*

AQABA OLD TOWN

Life continues here as it has for centuries. Stroll along the narrow alleys linking the markets where the locals come to shop. In the vegetable market the stalls are piled high with fruit and vegetables or large mounds of exotic spices. Elsewhere you can buy meat and fish and, if the smell of freshly baked bread and pastries gets too much to bear, pop into one of the small cafés.

border with Saudi Arabia. The Wadi Rum protected area is part of this desert and an area where visitors and outdoor enthusiasts can explore the vast expanse on foot, camel or in four-wheel-drive vehicles.

Serious climbers are attracted to this part of Jordan by the variety of scrambles and challenging climbs including the breathtaking Jebel Rum. Walkers can head out on the less strenuous routes and trails that go through the sand dunes, through sandstone hills and across dry desert.

AQABA ★★★

Aqaba is an ancient settlement dating back to 4000BCE. It grew up around a major junction of trading routes running between Asia, Africa and Europe. In biblical times **King Solomon** built ships on the shores of the **Red Sea** at **Ezion-Geber**. Archaeologists believe that during the Iron Age the port of Ezion-Geber stood where Aqaba now is. In the 10th century BCE the **Queen of Sheba** travelled here from **Jerusalem** to visit the court of King Solomon.

The World's Oldest Church ★

Archaeologists digging in Aqaba have unearthed what they believe to be the world's oldest purpose-built church. Constructed sometime in the late 3rd century CE, it is slightly older than the 4th-century **Church of the Holy Sepulchre** in **Jerusalem** and also the **Church of the Nativity** in **Bethlehem**. The remains of the church can be seen on a site east of **Istiqlal Street** near the parking area of the bus station.

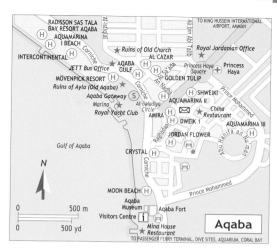

Islamic City of Ayla ★★

Opposite the **Mövenpick Resort** are the excavated remains of the walled city of **Ayla**. This was built during the early years of the **Islamic era** and is a rare example of early Islamic urbanization. Ayla benefited greatly from the annual **Hajj** pilgrimage to **Mecca**, particularly in years when the desert route was too dangerous. Then the route taken through Jordan was on the **King's Highway** which joined the Cairo Road at the Red Sea. A tetrapylon of four interconnecting arches stood at the centre of two intersecting axial streets which in turn led to the four main gates of the city. Ayla continued to prosper until the end of the 12th century CE when it went into decline following a series of Bedouin raids, Crusader attacks and earthquakes.

Excavations at Ayla were conducted from 1986–93 by a team from the Oriental Institute of the University of Chicago led by Associate Professor Donald Whitcom. Following their excavations the town was preserved as a tourist attraction. The archaeologists have designed a series of signs to guide visitors along the streets and to explain the significance of the excavated buildings.

AQABA FREE TRADE ZONE

This was created by the passing of the Aqaba Special Economic Zone Authority Law in August of 2000. Within its borders businesses have significant tax advantages. Although administered by a government-controlled authority, business within the zone is largely driven by private enterprise. Its aim is to attract significant investment to create an environmentally sustainable business development and a high-class tourist destination with the attraction of duty-free shopping.

Below: *Aqaba Fort was built originally by the Crusaders, rebuilt by the Mamelukes and captured by Lawrence and Feisal during the Great Arab Revolt.*

Aqaba Fort ★★★

This was the **Fortress of Helim** built by the **Crusaders** who occupied this area in the 12th century. During the 14th century **Qansah al-Ghouri**, one of the last of the Mameluke Sultans, had it rebuilt and it has since been considerably altered. When **Lawrence of Arabia** and **Prince Feisal** drove the Ottamans from Aqaba during the Great Arab Revolt, the **Hashemite Coat of Arms** was placed above the fort's main doorway. Open daily, 08:00–18:00 (17:00 on Fridays). A visit to the fort is included in the price of a ticket for the museum.

Museum ★★★

The building that houses the museum also contains the **Aqaba Visitors' Centre**. It was once the home of **Sharif Hussein bin Ali**, the great-great-grandfather of King Abdullah. The main collection in the museum is the mid-7th to 12th-century **Islamic period artefacts** recovered from the site of **Ayla**. Highlights include a hoard of **Fatimid dinars** minted at Sajilmasa in Morocco and a **Kufic inscription** from the Qu'ran that once surmounted the

eastern gate of the city. Other important items are the first milestone from the **Via Nova Traiana** and three **bronze Nabatean figurines** unearthed at Rum in 1998. Open daily, 08:00–18:00 (17:00 on Fridays). Admission charge.

Jordan Experience ★★★

This is a fantastic **3D multimedia theatre** located in the Aqaba Gateway shopping mall. The film is a twenty-minute journey by microlight aircraft. It covers the major highlights of Jordan including the **Dead Sea**, through the Siq at **Petra** and along the canyons of the **Wadi Rum**. The huge centre screen and two smaller side screens give a wrap-around effect. This creates the illusion that viewers are in the aircraft. The effect is further enhanced by a floor that tilts on hydraulic ramps to match the movement of the microlight.

Aquarium ★★

This is within the **Marine Science Station** which is out of town some 10km (6 miles) to the south. The **Red Sea** is rich in undersea life and the aquarium was built to let

Above: *One of the public beaches by the Promenade in Aqaba, with glass-bottomed boats waiting on the Red Sea.*

non-divers discover the importance of the coral reef ecosystem in the **Gulf of Aqaba**. It contains more than 30 species of coral, 30 types of invertebrate and over 45 species of reef fish. Most popular are the parrotfish and the moray eels. Divers will also find this a useful place to visit before venturing into the water. It's worth having a look at the poisonous stonefish in order to avoid them later in the wild. The aquarium also has a simulation of a coral reef in a giant roofless tank. Open daily, 08:00–17:00. Admission charge.

THE RED SEA ★★★

Snorkellers and **scuba divers** head for Aqaba in droves. With the water temperature averaging 23°C (73°F), diving and snorkelling are possible all year round. Add to that the mild water currents and lack of stormy weather and you have near perfect diving conditions. But that's only part of the reason why the Gulf of Aqaba is such a popular dive destination. Underwater there are 110 different species of soft coral, another 120 of the hard variety and over 1000 species of fish. Non-divers can also get in on the act. A fleet of **glass-bottomed boats** hug the beaches touting for passengers. This is a great way to explore the magical undersea world, but bargain hard and agree on a price before setting foot in the boat.

Beaches in Aqaba are either private or public. Most of the private beaches front the luxury hotels but non-guests can usually gain access to the facilities for a fee. The **Royal Diving Club** and the **Mövenpick Resort** both have excellent beaches.

The **public beach** runs from the Yacht Club along to the Fort. It is very popular with Jordanians. It is also noisy and congested. Head along here if you want to see what the locals do on holiday and take your lead from them. You'll see women sitting fully clothed in the shallow water. Women should take this as a clue. It is not a great idea to start sunbathing here or to go swimming in a scant western swimming costume.

WADI RUM – THE VALLEY OF THE MOON ★★★

The dramatic **desert** landscape of Wadi Rum was formed countless thousands of years ago when the earth's surface cracked. The extreme pressure that caused this also created the great **sandstone** and **granite ridges** that characterize the area. It looks in places like the surface of another planet, which is possibly why the Bedouin call it the **Valley of the Moon**.

ARAB BRIDGE FERRY TO EGYPT

It is possible to cross the Gulf of Aqaba to the Egyptian port of Nuweiba and from there travel south to the resort of Sharm el Sheik or arrange a trip to St Catherine's Monastery on the Sinai Peninsula. AB (Arab Bridge) Maritime run a fast one-hour ferry every day with the exception of Saturday. The ferry departs at 12:00. The return journey from Nuweiba leaves at 16:00. Bookings need to be made in advance.

Opposite: *The Red Sea is a diver's paradise.*
Below: *Wadi Rum, the Valley of the Moon.*

T E LAWRENCE

Thomas Edward Lawrence was the British Army liaison officer to the Arab forces during the **Great Arab Revolt**. Lawrence fought with the troops, raiding the Hejaz Railway, taking the port of Aqaba and capturing Damascus. His adoption of Arab customs and dress coupled with sensational publicity from the US journalist Lowell Thomas gave birth to the legend of Lawrence of Arabia.

Archaeologists have uncovered signs of people living here as far back as the **Neolithic** period of the 8th and 9th centuries BCE. Later it would become an important stop on the main **caravan trading routes** between Arabia, Syria and Palestine because of the availability of water. It is now home to several **Bedouin** tribes. Some have settled in the villages of Rum and Diseh while others still live deep in the desert in their traditional black goat's-hair tents.

Prince Feisal bin Hussein and T E Lawrence were based here for part of the time during the **Great Arab Revolt** in World War I.

Seven Pillars of Wisdom **

The one road into Wadi Rum branches off the Desert Highway. As you approach the visitors' centre you will see on the left a mountain, Jebel al-Mazmar, known locally as the Seven Pillars of Wisdom. It was allegedly given this name by **T E Lawrence** and was said to have been the inspiration for his book of the same name.

Below: *The Seven Pillars of Wisdom, supposedly the inspiration for the title of T E Lawrence's book.*

Unfortuately, the reality is that Lawrence had chosen that title for another book long before he came to Wadi Rum. It is a quote from the Book of Proverbs, 'Wisdom hath builded her house, she has hewn out her seven pillars.'

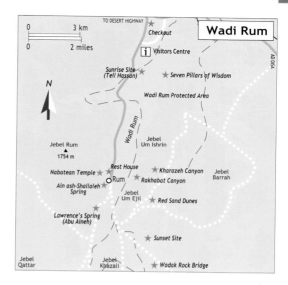

In Lawrence's personal account of the Great Arab Revolt he describes arriving at Wadi Rum: 'Day was still young as we rode between two great pikes of sandstone to the foot of a long, soft slope poured down from the domed hills in front of us. It was tamarisk-covered: the beginning of the Valley of Rumm, they said. We looked up on the left to a long wall of rock, sheering in like a thousand-foot wave towards the middle of the valley; whose other arc, to the right, was an opposing line of steep, red broken hills.'

Desert Patrol Fort ★★

There is an old fort by the side of the road leading into Wadi Rum. This was built some time in the 1930s and is the headquarters of the famous Desert Patrol. These men patrol the Eastern Desert on their camels wearing one of the world's most distinctive police uniforms. It consists of a long khaki dishdash with a red bandolier. Around the waist a belt attaches a holster and gun and a rather wicked-looking traditional dagger. Headwear is the traditional red and white *kouffieh* of the Jordanian Bedouin. The Desert Patrol troopers wrap this under their chins. They are happy to welcome visitors to their fort, share a cup of coffee with them and pose for photographs.

LAWRENCE OF ARABIA

Starring Peter O'Toole, David Lean's 1962 award-winning film on the life of T E Lawrence was mainly shot on location in the desert of Wadi Rum. It covers some of the major events of the Arab Revolt including the attacks on Aqaba, the Hejaz Railway and Damascus. Some terrible liberties were taken with the historical events, but Hollywood has never been known for letting the truth interfere with a good yarn. The scenery is, however, absolutely authentic and the film is worth viewing for that alone.

Visitors' Centre ★

The Visitors' Centre sits by the road opposite the 'Seven Pillars'. All of the land beyond it is part of the protected area. As well as a car park, the centre has tourist information services, restaurants and craft shops. You can hire a registered guide here as well as booking a variety of tours. Several options are available – you can take a one-hour trip by four-wheel-drive vehicle or camel to the nearest attractions, or you can go on a full-blown desert expedition taking several days. It is best to have made reservations with a chosen guide several days in advance. Visitors arriving without reservations can buy a ticket for their chosen tour and are then allocated the next driver or camel boy in the line. Open daily, 07:00–22:00. An admission fee is payable.

Rum Village ★

This is a very small settlement, with very limited accommodation for visitors, lying about 7km (4 miles) beyond the visitors' centre. There is a **Government Rest House**, a few small shops selling basic provisions and a handful of restaurants selling inexpensive Arab dishes.

Nabatean Temple ★

This temple is a short walk from the Rest House in Rum village. It was built sometime around the 1st to the 2nd century CE. The columns and walls are covered in Nabatean inscriptions.

Lawrence's Spring ★

A short distance from Rum village is the spring where Lawrence washed off the dust of the desert.

'I went straight up the gully into the face of the hill, along the ruined wall of the conduit by which a spout of water had once run down the ledges to a Nabatean well-house on the valley floor. It was a climb of fifteen minutes to a tired person, and not difficult. At the top, the waterfall, el Shellala as the Arabs named it, was only a few yards away.'

Some **Nabatean inscriptions** can be seen cut into the rock above the spring.

Jebel Rum ★★

This is the **highest mountain** in Jordan and attracts a number of climbing enthusiasts. It's a strenuous ten-hour round trip to the summit and should only be undertaken by people having the necessary level of skills and fitness. Even then a local guide should be used. The entire protected area is a Mecca for climbers and trekkers but great care has to be taken when venturing into the desert alone. Plenty of food and water must be taken, a route plan, including an estimated time of completion, should be left with someone, and a compass is essential. Di

---

SHARIF ALI

Hussein bin Ali was Sharif of Mecca at the outbreak of World War I. British promises of an autonomous Arab Empire after the war led him to switch his allegiance from the Ottoman Turks and initiate the Great Arab Revolt. His son Abdullah became Emir of Transjordan after the war. Faisal, another son, was briefly King of Syria until the French took over, then he became King of Iraq.

BALLOON TRIPS

There is nothing to compare with rising just before dawn in the desert, watching the sun come up, then gently lifting off in a hot-air balloon to soar across the mountains, canyons and sand dunes. The **Royal Aero Sports Club of Jordan** who organize the trips are based at King Hussein International Airport in Aqaba. They also offer skydiving, tandem jumps over the Gulf of Aqaba, and can arrange small-plane trips over Petra.

Opposite: *Go camel trekking through the moonscape scenery of the Wadi Rum and create your own version of 'Lawrence of Arabia'.*

Taylor and Tony Howard's *Walks and Scrambles in Wadi Rum* and *Jordan Walks, Treks, Caves, Climbs and Canyons* are a couple of books detailing the various walks and climbs, and are essential reading for experienced people wanting to go it alone. Di and Tony have walked and climbed extensively throughout Jordan and in Wadi Rum.

The Desert ★★★

T E Lawrence described the desert of Wadi Rum as 'vast, echoing and Godlike'. Massive mountains of red, brown, yellow and white sandstone flank wide canyons. From this sandstone nature has, over the millennia, carved interesting **geological formations** including arches and bridges.

This is one of Jordan's main tourist attractions and to preserve it the government declared it a protected area in 1998. It is managed by local people under the umbrella of the **Royal Society for the Conservation of Nature**.

Below: *The Bedouin of Wadi Rum still live in goat's-hair tents and make their living raising goats, sheep and camels.*

The Bedouin ★★★

Wadi Rum is inhabited by Bedouin of the **Humeitat** and **Mzanah** tribes. Although many of them have moved into the concrete houses of Rum, several still

live a nomadic life in the desert. They still dress in the traditional way, observe the old customs and live in goat's-hair tents. They make their living by raising goats, sheep and camels and from tourism. The Bedouin have an ancient code of offering **hospitality** to travellers and there is no finer experience in the desert than

being invited into a tent to share a meal or a glass of mint tea or cardamom-flavoured coffee.

Above: *Many Bedouin still live a nomadic life in the desert.*

Flora and Fauna ★★★

Wadi Rum is home to several rare plants and animals. The interested visitor can seek out many rare species of plants and herbs and, with a suitable guide, can learn about the plants used by the Bedouin for their medicinal properties. Red anemones grow by the roadside and black iris can also be found. Ibex have been spotted in the desert, as well as the sand cat, grey wolf, Blandford's fox and the very rare red fox. Look out too for hedgehogs, porcupine and the striped hyena.

Bird-watchers can see the Sinai rose finch, as well as wheatears, the brown-necked raven, buzzards, griffon vultures, sparrows and the very rare Verreaux's eagle. From the insect world there is an interesting spider called the camel-spider by the Bedouin. They fear it because it can harm their camels. It is not, however, dangerous to humans.

Aqaba and the Southeastern Desert at a Glance

BEST TIMES TO VISIT

Aqaba is a year-round resort with ten hours of sun in the winter, temperatures rarely falling below 21°C (70°F) and little or no rainfall. The summer months (May–August) have temperatures of 35–40°C (95–104°F), between 11 and 13 hours of sunshine and absolutely no rain.

GETTING THERE

There are several ways to enter Aqaba. Most visitors to Jordan will arrive in Amman and then take the bus or a hire car for the five-hour drive south on the Desert Highway. **Royal Wings** operates a daily shuttle service from Amman to Aqaba airport. Aqaba airport is also the arrival point for several charter flights from Europe and elsewhere. It is also possible to enter Jordan at Aqaba, especially if arriving from Egypt. The **Fast Ferry** that plies the Gulf of Aqaba between Egypt and Jordan departs from the terminal at the port of Aqaba at 13:00 every day except Saturday, and arrives at Nuweiba on the Sinai Peninsula by 14:00. The return ferry leaves Nuweiba at 16:00 and docks in Aqaba an hour later. The **Slow Ferries** depart from the same points, leaving Aqaba at midnight and arriving in Nuweiba at 03:00. The return trip from Nuweiba leaves at midnight and should arrive in

Aqaba by 03:00. All times are approximate and delays are commonplace. Passengers should arrive at least one hour prior to the sailing time. For further information, tel: 03 201 3236, www.abmaritime.com.jo

GETTING AROUND

Aqaba is small enough to explore on foot but there are plenty of taxis that can be hailed in the street. Aqaba bus station is in the centre of the town and from there buses run to Amman, Tafileh, Petra and Wadi Rum. Buses to Al-Karak don't leave from the station but from a nearby street (ask for directions at the station). The route of this bus is along the road to the Dead Sea via As Safi and this is one way to visit Lot's cave sanctuary and its soon-to-open new museum by public transport. It is also possible to visit Petra and Wadi Rum by joining an organized tour or by hiring a taxi for the day.

WHERE TO STAY

Aqaba

LUXURY

Mövenpick Resort & Residence Aqaba, King Hussein Street, Aqaba 77110, tel: 03 203 4020, www.moevenpick-hotels.com/en/pub/your_hotels/worldmap/aqaba/overview.cfm? One of the finest hotels in the south of Jordan, with direct

access to its own private beach and unbelievable views over the Red Sea and the Gulf of Aqaba. **Radisson SAS Tala Bay Resort Aqaba**, PO Box 982, Aqaba 77110, tel: 03 209 0777, www.radissonblu.com/resort-aqaba Large luxury hotel resort with private beach and first-class service.

MID-RANGE

Al Cazar Hotel, PO Box 2624, Aqaba 77110, tel: 03 201 3735, www.alcazarhotel.com City-centre hotel located within five minutes' walk of the local amenities, restaurants and shops.

Coral Bay

Royal Diving Club, located 16km (10 miles) south of Aqaba, tel: 03 201 5555, www.rdc.jo A first-class private beach and access to the coral reef makes this a prime location for divers and snorkellers. It also has a splendid restaurant and can be reached cheaply by taxi or by using the hotel's shuttle bus.

BUDGET

Several hotels are clustered together in the backstreets of Aqaba town centre near the post office. The best of the bunch are:

Amira Hotel, tel: 03 201 8840. Clean, simple rooms in a good location.

Dweik Hotel, tel: 03 203 5919, www.dweikhotel2.com Clean and comfortable and with TV in each room.

Wadi Rum

Accommodation is scarce and best booked well in advance. If you intend spending more than one day in Rum it is a good idea to pre-book with one of the local guides and they will take care of food and accommodation. Spending the night deep in the desert in one of the Bedouin camps is the experience of a lifetime and, while showers and toilets are not great, the food, hospitality and atmosphere more than compensate. Saleem Ali of Jordan Tracks (www.jordantracks. com) is highly recommended. Basic accommodation for visitors is available at:
Bait Ali, just off the main road to Rum village, mobile: +962 79 5548133, www.baitali.com Modern camp site with traditional-style Bedouin tents, facilities and nightly entertainment.
Rum Rest House, on the right as you enter Rum village, tel: 03 201 8867. Advance booking is recommended.

Aqaba

Captain's Restaurant, behind the Corniche beside the Aquamarina II City, tel: 03 206 0710. Fish fresh from the Red Sea as well as salads, standard Arab fare and pasta.

Red Sea Grill, Mövenpick Resort & Residence Aqaba, tel: 03 203 4020. This is an open-air seafood restaurant overlooking the beach. It's as good as eating gets in Aqaba.
Royal Yacht Club, behind the Aqaba Gateway Mall, tel: 03 202 2404. Superb Italian dishes, freshly caught fish cooked to perfection and sweets to seriously damage your waistline.
Mina House, south of Aqaba Fort by the fishing harbour, tel: 03 201 2699. Very busy floating restaurant in a former tug boat. Seafood is naturally a speciality and the squid is particularly fine. They also serve barbecued meat.

Wadi Rum

There is a reasonable selection of eateries serving basic Arab food near the Rest House.

Abercrombie & Kent Jordan, Abdullah Bin Abbas Street, opposite Orchid's Hotel, Amman, tel: 06 566 5465, www.akdmc.com
Al-Thuraya Travel & Tours, PO Box 1883, Amman

11821, tel: 06 553 5525, www.althurayatravel.net
Jordan Tracks, PO Box 468, Aqaba, tel: 7964 82801, www.jordantracks.com Saleem Ali and his family operate the only Bedouin-owned tourist agency in Jordan, based in Wadi Rum. Besides tours of Wadi Rum, they also organize tours and excursions throughout Jordan.
Nyazi Tours – Eco Tourism, Al-Warethlany Street, Aqaba 77110, tel: 03 202 2801, www.nyazi.com.jo

Emergency calls, tel: 196.
British Embassy, tel: 06 590 9200.
US Embassy, tel: 06 590 6000.
Al-Khalidi Medical Centre, tel: 06 464 4281.
Tourism Development Board Office, Queen Alia International Airport, Amman, tel: 06 445 2063.
Jordan Tourist Board, Amman, tel: 06 567 8294.
Royal Society for the Conservation of Nature (RSCN), tel: 06 533 7931.
Sale Tax Return Office, Queen Alia International Airport, tel: 06 445 1552.

AQABA	J	F	M	A	M	J	J	A	S	O	N	D
AVERAGE TEMP. °F	70	70	77	86	95	100	104	102	97	90	79	72
AVERAGE TEMP. °C	21	21	25	30	35	38	40	39	36	32	26	22
RAINFALL in	0.4	0.4	0.2	0	0	0	0	0	0	0.4	0.4	0.4
RAINFALL mm	10	10	5	0	0	0	0	0	0	10	10	10
DAYS OF RAINFALL	1	1	1	0	0	0	0	0	0	1	1	1

Travel Tips

Tourist Information
Jordan Tourism Board,
PO Box 830688, Amman
11183, tel: 06 567 8444,
fax: 06 567 8295,
www.visitjordan.com
Main Overseas Offices:
Germany: Kleber PR
Network GmbH, Hamburger
Alee 45, 60486 Frankfurt,
tel: (49 69) 71 91 36 62,
fax: (49 69) 71 91 36 51.
Italy: Open Mind
Consulting, Piazza Santa
Giulia 11, 10124 Torino,
tel: (39 11) 811 5249,
fax: (39 11) 812 8633.
Holland: Jordan Tourism
Board Benelux,
Nieuwendammerkade 26G,
1022 AB Amsterdam, tel:
(31 20) 670 5211, fax:
(31 20) 670 5357.
United Kingdom:
Jordan Tourism Board UK,
The Brighter Group, The Pod,
London's Vertical Gateway,
Bridges Court Road, London
SW11 3BE, tel: (44 20) 7223
1878, fax: (44 20) 7326 9890,
http://uk.visitjordan.com
USA: Jordan Tourism
Board North America,
6867 Elm Street, Suite 102,
McLean, VA 22101,
tel: (1 703) 243 7404,
fax: (1 703) 243 7406,
http://na.visitjordan.com

Entry Requirements
All visitors need a passport,
valid for six months from the
date of entry, and a visa.
Citizens of the UK, USA,
Australia, Canada and
European Union Countries
can obtain their visa on
arrival at the airport.
A single-entry tourist visa
obtained in advance from an
embassy or consulate is valid
for three months and can be
extended at any police station
in Jordan. Visas issued at
the airport are only valid for
15 days and can also be
extended at police stations.
Registration at any police
station is also a requirement
for any stay exceeding two
weeks. Visitors arriving via
the Aqaba Special Economic
Zone will be issued with a
free one-day visa. While
this is valid for travel anywhere in the country, it
can only be extended at the
ASEZ office in Aqaba.

Customs
Personal items including
cameras, clothes, computers
and video cameras for
personal use are exempt
from duty. In addition, any-
one over the age of 18 can
import the following goods:
200 cigarettes or 25 cigars or
200g of tobacco; 1litre of
alcohol; a couple of opened
bottles of perfume and eau
de Cologne or lotion in
opened bottles for personal
use only; gifts totalling JD50
or US$150.

Health Requirements
Jordan does not require any
health certificates on entry
unless you are arriving from a
country infected with yellow
fever and cholera. It is advisable to have inoculations for
tetanus, typhoid, polio and
hepatitis before arriving.

Getting There
By Air: Most visitors arrive by
air. Amman's Queen Alia
International (AMM) has sched-
uled flights to and from most
countries. Royal Jordanian
Airlines is the national airline.

By Ferry: There is a daily car and passenger ferry and a high-speed hydrofoil from Nuweiba in Egypt to Jordan's only port, Aqaba.

What to Pack

Evenings can be cool all year round so bring a sweater or a jacket. The winter months from November to March are wet as well as cold so warm and waterproof clothing is essential. Shorts, T-shirts and swimwear are good for the beach and don't forget sunglasses, sunscreen and a wide-brimmed hat. Away from the beach loose-fitting, casual cotton clothes, trousers and long-sleeved shirts are acceptable. A pair of comfortable walking shoes or boots or good quality trekking sandals will be required for exploring the ancient ruins and deserts. A suit, shirt and tie is the norm for business attire. Women should avoid short skirts, shorts, sleeveless blouses, backless dresses or anything see-through or tight-fitting. The dress code in Jordan is very conservative and a lot of what is fashionable in the western world would be considered provocative or even obscene there.

Money Matters

Currency: The unit of currency is the Jordanian Dinar (JD). It is divided into 100 piastres or 1000 fils. Notes come in denominations of JD50, 20, 10, 5 and 1. There is also a 500 fils note. Coins are JD1, ½ and ¼; 10, 5, 2 and ½ piastres.

Exchange: Banking hours are Saturday–Thursday, 08:30–15:00. During Ramadan banks open from 08:30–10:00 but some may remain open for the afternoon. Foreign currency and travellers' cheques issued by UK and USA banks can be exchanged in all banks, bureaux de change and most of the larger hotels. Shop around for the best deals. Money-changers in town centres tend to offer better deals to attract custom while hotels should only be used if there are no other options. ATMs are now readily available in all of the large towns and throughout the capital. Most of the international cards are accepted including Visa, MasterCard, Diners Club and American Express. Cards are also generally accepted in hotels, restaurants and larger shops in Amman and the larger towns. In smaller shops and off the beaten track carry sufficient cash to cover your expenses for at least a couple of days.

Tipping: Taxi drivers don't get tips but it is customary to round the fare up. Some hotels and restaurants add a 10–12% service charge to the bill. Where there is no charge, tips will be appreciated. There is no set amount and you should leave what you want but never more than 10%.

Accommodation

Accommodation in Jordan can be surprisingly cheap. Even the large luxury hotels will cost less than their equivalent in Europe. Standards vary from a thin mattress on a flat roof for a few coins to the seriously luxurious Kempinski Ishtar Dead Sea Resort where there is one suite that runs to five figures. Government rest houses and backpacker hostels provide very good value. Most have basic but clean rooms with the availability of hot showers. In winter, getting a room with central heating is a distinct advantage, as is a room with air conditioning in the height of summer.

CONVERSION CHART

FROM	TO	MULTIPLY BY
Millimetres	Inches	0.0394
Centimetres	Inches	0.3937
Metres	Yards	1.0936
Metres	Feet	3.281
Kilometres	Miles	0.6214
Square kilometres	Square miles	0.386
Hectares	Acres	2.471
Litres	Pints	1.760
Kilograms	Pounds	2.205
Tonnes	Tons	0.984

To convert Celsius to Fahrenheit: x 9 ÷ 5 + 32

Eating Out

The cuisine varies from simple, traditional Arab fare to exotic international dishes. While there are several fine restaurants that could easily hold their own on the world stage there is nothing to compare with eating in a small restaurant full of locals. You can learn a lot about a country by eating the local food and it needn't cost the earth.

Meze: order a selection of these as a starter and share them with friends.

Hummus: chickpeas blended with tahina and a little added lemon juice and garlic.

Vine Leaves: stuffed with a meat or rice mixture seasoned with herbs and spices.

Baba ghanoush: aubergines cooked over charcoal and then pulped. Very tasty.

Tabouleh: fresh salad of tomatoes, spring onions, parsley and mint mixed with bulgur wheat.

Musakhan: very tasty dish of roasted chicken in olive oil and onion sauce served on flat Arab bread.

Mensaf: eat this with your hand. Stewed lamb and yoghurt sauce on a bed of rice.

Maqhloubey: this means upside down. It is lumps of cooked fish, lamb and chicken mixed with rice then pressed into a mould and turned out upside down.

Baklava: a seriously sweet and sticky desert made from layers of filo pastry with pine nuts and honey.

Ataif: deep-fried pancakes full of white cheese or nuts and covered with syrup. Unfortunately you will only come across them during Ramadan.

Coffee: Arab coffee can be an acquired taste. Small cups of very strong coffee are served with a sludge of grounds at the bottom.

Sahlab: This hot milk drink is served with pistachios and cinnamon and rose water. It is made from the sahlab root, hence the name.

Transport

Air: Royal Jordanian's subsidiary, Royal Wings, operates a daily shuttle from Amman to Aqaba.

Buses: The big towns and Amman are all connected by a reasonably efficient bus service. There are three bus companies all running modern coaches with air conditioning: Alpha (tel: 06 585 0626), JETT (tel: 06 566 4146) and Trust International Transport (tel: 06 581 3427).

Car Hire: Most major hire companies have a presence in Amman and Aqaba. Local companies often provide the best deals. Cars with drivers can also be hired by the day or half-day from most major hotels and travel agents.

Driving: Although national driving licences are accepted (provided they were issued at least a year before travel), an international driving licence is recommended. Rental cars have different number plates from those of Jordanians. Foreign nationals are not allowed to drive vehicles with normal Jordanian plates unless they hold a Jordanian driving licence. Driving is on the right and speed limits are 60kph (37mph) in towns and cities, 80kph (50mph) on main roads and 120kph (75mph) on motorways. One thing to watch out for are the sleeping policemen (speed bumps) in towns and villages. They are mostly unmarked, and hitting them at any sort of speed can be a bone-jarring experience.

With the exception of Amman (which can be a challenge owing to the lack of street signs), driving in Jordan is fairly straight-forward. Main roads are well surfaced and modern. This is not the case out in the desert where wandering off the major roads leads to minor roads (in various stages of decomposition) and tracks. Do not venture onto these without a high clearance four-wheel-drive vehicle. If you plan on driving on desert tracks, make sure the vehicle is in good repair, the tank is full of petrol, carry plenty of water, a supply of food, map and compass. Better still, hire a local guide who knows the area well. In a breakdown or emergency contact the Royal Automobile Club of Jordan, tel: 06 585 0626.

Taxis: These are metered and relatively inexpensive. They can also be hired by the day or half-day. Share-taxis are licensed and operate on a fixed route with a standard price scale. They pick up and set down anywhere along their route. Share-taxis can be booked in advance via hotels and travel agencies for trips to tourist attractions including Petra.

Trains: There is no public rail transport in Jordan.

Business Hours

Avoid making appointments for Fridays. Normal office hours are Sunday–Thursday 09:30–13:30 and 15:30–18:00. Government office hours are Sunday–Thursday 08:00–15:00. During Ramadan these hours are reduced.

Time Difference

Jordan is two hours ahead of Greenwich Mean Time (GMT).

Communications

Most of the large towns and cities have public telephones that use prepaid phone cards. These can be purchased from shops or travel agencies. Mobile phone coverage is good and Internet is widely available in hotels and Internet cafés. Many of the less expensive hotels like the Mariam in Madaba offer free wireless connection. The luxury hotels, on the other hand, charge mercilessly for this service.

Electricity

Current is 220–240 volts. Plugs are generally two-pin European standard, although there may be a few British three-pin outlets left. With the appropriate adaptor most European appliances will work in Jordan. Visitors from the USA will need a transformer as well as an adaptor to avoid damage to their appliances.

Weights and Measures

Jordan uses the metric system.

Health Precautions

Although Jordan is one of the cleaner countries in the Middle East, a few precautions are advisable until your digestive system gets used to the change. Drink only bottled water. The top-end hotels have their own filtration systems so their water is safe enough to drink. When eating fruit make sure it is well washed first. Avoid cold meats and salads that may have been sitting on a buffet

table for a long time, particularly during summer.

Media

English-language papers include the daily *Jordan Times* and *The Star* which is a weekly. A number of daily newspapers are published in Arabic. These include *Al Ra'y*, *Al Arab al Yawm* and *Ad Dustour*. Jordan Radio and Television is the state-run broadcaster operating three terrestrial channels and Jordan Satellite Channel. Channel One is the main network, Two is the sports network and Three is for films. Radio services are broadcast in Arabic and English. Mood FM and Play 99.6 are two independent radio stations broadcasting pop music.

Personal Safety

Jordan is a very safe country but there have been some terrorist attacks since 2001. In September 2006 a tourist was killed in a shooting incident in Amman. The previous year suicide bombers killed 60 people, mainly Jordanians, at three Amman hotels. Having said that, you have a better chance of winning the lottery than getting killed in a terrorist attack. To put terrorism in perspective, consider that while some 3000 people lost their lives on 9/11, nearly 17,000 US citizens were destroyed in the same year by drunken drivers. Security has been beefed up and all the top-range hotels have metal detectors and security guards. It takes a few minutes to get into the hotel but this minor inconvenience is repaid by a feeling of well being. Take a few basic precautions when out on your own. Don't flash large wads of cash about and don't wander down dimly lit alleys at night. Women travelling on their own are as safe in Jordan as anywhere else but they should wear sensible, loose-fitting clothing covering the arms and legs and the nape of the neck. Don't sit in the front seat of taxis.

Emergencies

Police, tel: 191
Ambulance, tel: 199
Fire Brigade, tel: 199
Traffic Police, tel: 190
International Telephone Operator, tel: 0132
Directory enquiries, tel: 195

Best Buys

Bedouin rugs make great practical souvenirs. They can be purchased from the Bani Hamida House (tel: 06 465 8696) just off Rainbow Street near the First Circle in Amman, from the Bani Hamida centre in Mukawir, or from many of the shops in Madaba. Hebron handmade glass is now made in Jordan by a family that came originally from Hebron. You'll find it in many of the souvenir shops in Amman and Madaba. Gold is surprisingly cheap and sold by weight. Haggle for bargains in the Gold Souq in Amman. The ubiquitous glass bottles filled with coloured sand are available throughout Jordan. Prices and quality vary considerably so shop around. Pottery with Arabic script design has become very popular. Bowls, plates and vases are all worth consideration. These can be bought direct from the workshops that produce them. Silsal Pottery (tel: 06 593 1128) is down a street to the right between the fifth and fourth circles, and Hazem Zoubi's gallery (tel: 06 568 0908) is behind the Safeway supermarket in Shumaysani. You can also find pottery and a number of other souvenirs at Al-Aydi (tel: 06 464 4555) behind the second circle in Jebel Amman.

GOOD READING

Asher, Michael (1998) *Lawrence: The Uncrowned King of Arabia*. Penguin Books Ltd, London, New York.
Carter, Jimmy (2006) *Palestine: Peace Not Apartheid*. Simon and Schuster, New York, London.
Dawood, NJ (translator) (1990) *The Koran*. Penguin Books, London, New York.
Fisk, Robert (2006) *The Great War For Civilization*. Harper Perennial, London, New York.
Lawrence, TE (1997) *The Seven Pillars of Wisdom*. Wordsworth Editions, Hertfordshire, England.
Lunt, James (1984) *Glubb Pasha: A Biography*. Harper Collins, London.
Lunt, James (1989) *Hussein of Jordan: A Political Biography*. Macmillan, London.
Paula, Christa; Saunders, David; Khammash, Ammar (2005) *Jordan: A Timeless Land*. I B Tauris & Co Ltd, London, New York.
Salibi, Kamal (1998) *The Modern History of Jordan*. I B Tauris & Co Ltd, London, New York.
Taylor, Di; Howard, Tony (1999) *Jordan: Walks, Treks, Caves, Climbs, Canyons in Pella, Ajlun, Moab, Dana, Petra and Rum*. Cicerone Press, Milnthorp, Cumbria, England.
Thomas, Lowell (2002) *With Lawrence in Arabia*. Prion Books Ltd, London.
Wallach, Janet (1996) *Desert Queen: The Extraordinary Life of Gertrude Bell*. Phoenix, London.

INDEX

Note: Numbers in **bold** indicate photographs